D1201058

Politics and Evangelism

Politics and Evangelism

PHILIPPE MAURY

It is not necessary to hope in order to undertake
nor to succeed in order to persevere.

ATTRIBUTED TO WILLIAM THE SILENT

DOUBLEDAY & CO., INC.

GARDEN CITY, NEW YORK

60-658

Translated by Marguerite Wieser from the French "Evangélisation et Politique," Editions Labor et Fides, 1958 (revised). A shorter presentation of the substance of this book has been prepared by the author and published in England by the Lutterworth Press as part of a series produced by the World Council of Churches.

CONTENTS

62

FOREWORD

This little book is a translation and adaptation of a French book with a similar title born of lectures given in 1957 at the Protestant Study Center in Geneva. It is not my intention here to present a systematic study of the subject of evangelism and politics. Rather, what I have undertaken is, in a way, a self-examination. For many years I have been both concerned with political problems and involved in evangelistic work. Like all students, before the Second World War, I was passionately interested in political problems, but it was only with the outbreak of war and especially the Nazi occupation of France that I was compelled to make political choices in which my whole life was at stake, not only because they were dangerous choices made under a totalitarian regime, but above all because my Christian integrity was called in question. After the liberation of France I was for almost a year in governmental service, and again I had to face hard, sometimes existential, decisions.

Back in those days I had already begun to think seriously about the relation between politics and evangelism. Out of this reflection came a small book, published by the World's Student Christian Federation and edited by Andreas Shanke and myself. Both of us had taken part in underground activities, he in Norway, I in France. This book, called *Christian Witness in the Resistance*, was a collection of personal testimonies from members of European student Christian movements. Its title was taken from the well-known French underground publication, issued jointly by Catholics and Protestants, *Les Cahiers du Témoinage Chrétien* (Journal of Christian Witness), which carried information about the struggle of all churches against National Socialism and called Christians to active resistance. This magazine actually did a first-class job of evangelism.

Since 1945, I have been on the staff of the World's Student Christian Federation. This means, first, that I have been living and working among students. One cannot live with students without entering into their preoccupation—I would say almost their obsession—with politics. More than anyone else students, indeed the whole university world, are subject to the fluctuations and the political upheavals of our time. By its very nature and tasks the academic community is a sensitive social sounding board. Like all young people, students suffer from the insecurity, the anxiety, the discouragement provoked by ideological confusion, international tension, economic crises, and atomic threat. But as intellectuals they feel more painfully their own helplessness in the face of political forces whose pawns they seem to be. Their studies also place them in the very storm center of the contemporary cultural crisis, and every day they can point to political causes and effects in all of this. Political forces assail them on all sides. They cannot escape, even though they seek refuge in science or art, even though they withdraw into contemplation and the search for personal purity. There is no ivory tower, sealed off, where a man could really ignore his political existence.

My work with the World's Student Christian Federation has meant, secondly, that I have tried to serve an ecumenical organization primarily concerned with evangelism. We live in a time when the church is again becoming aware of the importance and urgency of its missionary task. Almost everywhere in the world today the Christian community is waking up to the fact that, short of real renewal manifested once more in a victorious faith, the Church—from a human point of view—is doomed to death. Everywhere the Church is confronted by new pagan religions, through the renascence of ancient religions in Asia and elsewhere or in modern totalitarian ideologies. Everywhere, also, a biblical and theological renewal is making clear the centrality of Christ in the Christian message, compelling the Church to manifest itself in its true nature, which cannot be reduced to any human wisdom (be it philosophical, religious, or political), and giving the Church a fresh missionary impulse. Everywhere theologians, evangelists, youth movements, and church bodies are seeking to formulate both a theology and a methodology for evangelism which is at once faithful to the gospel and appropriate to the modern world.

All this has led me to ask myself questions about the relationship between politics and evangelism, and, as I have said, these pages are very much a self-examination: they aim to scrutinize what I have thought and done in the light of the biblical revelation and of the teaching of the Church. They make no pretense to be a systematic study. I am not a professional theologian but a layman. In writing this book I have hoped that it might be useful to men and women in the Church who, like myself, are concerned with the problems posed for them by politics and who are groping for the way to fulfill their evangelistic responsibility in faithfulness for the sake of the world.

PHILIPPE MAURY

Geneva, Switzerland
September, 1959

INTRODUCTORY NOTES

1. The theologians distinguish generally between three fundamental and permanent functions of the Church: *marturia, diakonia,* and *koinonia.* The first is witness or proclamation of the gospel; the second is service, charitable and social; and the third is the fellowship or communion of members of the Church with one another. Should we identify evangelization with *marturia*? I do not think so. Evangelization as we shall see is both proclamation and demonstration of the gospel, and therefore arises from all three functions of the Church. *Marturia, diakonia,* and *koinonia* all contribute to evangelism. All three have a missionary intention and scope. I certainly do not want to say that evangelism sums up the whole of these three tasks of the Church. But in the course of this study on the relationship between evangelism and politics, I shall speak of evangelism in a sense that goes far beyond the term *marturia* and tends to fusion with the idea of the Church's mission in the world and of the Church's responsibility toward the world.

2. The use of the word "church" has at all times raised problems of semantics. Can we legitimately speak of the Church when we have in mind now the body of Christ, now the totality of Christians in the world, now the local congregations, the confessions or the denominations? If we limit ourselves strictly to the New Testament use of the term, we would have to employ the word "church" only for the mystical and ecumenical reality of the body of Christ or for the local congregations or parishes. I think it is of no help to cling to a biblical purism. With or without theological justification, the term is currently used to cover many meanings. Each particular case therefore calls for a definition of the meaning in which the word is used. I propose to speak in the following chapters of the

13

Church (with a capital C) when I refer to that reality whose existence we confess in the Apostles' Creed. I shall speak of the church (with a small c) in relation to the local congregation or parish, the collective number of those who declare themselves Christians in the world or in one of its regions in a given moment of history. Lastly, with reference to confessional groupings, denominations, national churches, I shall employ the term with a small c and often, of course, in the plural, except when quoting the official title of a particular church.

Politics and Evangelism

CHAPTER I

Political Obstacles to Evangelism

I. THE CRISIS IN EVANGELIZATION

A church which ceases to evangelize is not only unfaithful to its Lord, but in fact ceases to be the Church of Jesus Christ. I will begin with this thesis. A church, for instance, which finds within itself the object of its mission, concentrating exclusively or even primarily on its theology, its administrative structures, its methods of Christian education, and its own fellowship, would not only be a scandal. Such a church condemns itself to death. Experience has shown that a church which neglects its missionary task is bound not only to decline in numbers but also to founder in spiritual stagnation which in the end is fatal.

In this mid-twentieth century we may legitimately ask ourselves the question: Are our churches not losing their sense of mission in the world? Are they not already terribly neglecting their evangelistic task?

PERSECUTION

In discussing the crisis in the mission of the church I am not referring to increasing material difficulties which our churches must so often face. We are all too much inclined to put the blame on government or society, those actual or potential persecutors of the Church. True, at the present time examples are plentiful of totalitarian regimes which threaten not only the mission of the Church but its very essence. Whether they are confronted with the great political ideologies of today—communism or fascism—or with the ancient religions of Asia which today are again on the march with both religious and nationalistic thrusts, or whether confronted even with the scandalous persecutions either initiated or tolerated by the Roman Catholic Church and, alas, by some Protestant churches as well, almost everywhere in the world Christians are up against increasing difficulties in carrying out their mission.

In many instances governments or society are prepared to tolerate the existence of small Christian communities, provided they refrain from any attempt to witness and win followers. Reluctant permission may be given to the holding of private worship services behind the closed doors of a church building which is as inconspicuous as possible. But as soon as the church seeks to break out of this ghetto, persecution sets in. Such is the experience of the church in Fascist, Communist, or Islamic countries. In some Islamic countries, for instance, evangelizing the faithful is subject to the death penalty; the lives of converted Moslems have often been threatened by former fellow believers, even when the converts had settled in the West. Persecution, however, does not necessarily proceed so brutally and publicly. There are many other weapons to force the church into walling itself up in a ministry which renounces any impact on the world and takes refuge in a disincarnate spirituality. These are certainly political obstacles to evangelism. Yet I for my part refuse to consider them as the true obstacles which explain the serious missionary crisis of today.

INDIFFERENCE

What, then, is the principal obstacle to effective evangelism in our time? Is it perhaps a widespread indifference that blocks the church's missionary action? In the West in particular our contemporaries seem to be vaccinated against the gospel and therefore immune to its proclamation. It does not matter so much whether this indifference is clothed in aggressive hostility or in plain apathy. The result is the same. I am thinking at this point of our French history during the past two centuries, marked as it has been by the progressive dechristianization of the whole of society. The eighteenth century witnessed the aristocracy, the higher bourgeoisie (the upper-middle class), and the intellectuals turning away from the church and the Christian faith. In the nineteenth century the contagion reached the remaining bourgeoisie, the people in rural areas, and the industrial workers. The return of one part of the bourgeoisie to the fold, for political reasons to be explained later, did not significantly change the general climate of anticlerical and even anti-Christian attitudes right up to the Second World War. This growing secularization is closely linked to the political and social history of France. Is the reason for our evangelistic failure, therefore, some intellectual or moral perversion to which the French people have yielded for the last two centuries? Is it the fault of the French people, or of the evil masters they followed, that the churches of France are not truly mindful of their mission?

THE GUILT OF THE CHURCH

I am convinced that it would be a mistake both spiritually and historically to explain the present evangelistic failure by the influence of social dogmas or systems, and by fateful political developments. Whatever the role of these social doctrines or systems, the responsibility for the crisis rests primarily with the church itself. The gravity of the situation lies in the church's indifference to its evangelistic calling. While there are indeed encouraging signs of renewal, our churches too often consider evangelism as the specialized task of a few experts, especially the clergy. Instead of understanding the task of evangelization as the very *raison d'être* of the Church, they view it as a minor task, as a superfluous activity, certainly much less important than church organization or the deepening of their own spiritual life. Our churches grow more and more interested in themselves and indifferent to the world.

Why this crisis? Once again I do not think that persecution or agnosticism are to be blamed. Persecution, hostility, indifference are after all the normal situation in the world for the Church of Jesus Christ, as foretold by the Lord himself. Far from endangering the Church and hindering its evangelistic ministry, opposition confers upon it new strength, new vitality, and new effectiveness. Nothing else but the persecutions of the Roman Empire made possible the rapid conquest of the Mediterranean world in the first century. And all the churches which today suffer from brutal persecution give to the others an example of a ministry which is not only courageous, but conquering.

The reasons for the present missionary crisis lie therefore within the church. They are spiritual and theological. If the church no longer knows how to announce the gospel to the world, it is because it forgets to be the Church of Jesus Christ; because it allows itself to be enslaved by the world; because it lives in isolation from the world; because, first and last, it has forgotten what task God gave it to perform in the world.

II. THE CHURCH, PRISONER OF THE WORLD

Let us try honestly to listen to the criticisms leveled against the church by our contemporaries and more specifically by modern religions and ideologies. The basic accusation recurs like a chorus. The church has allowed itself to become the tool of the dominant political and social forces: the church, Christianity itself, is indeed the "opiate of the people," which the powerful of this world use for the consolidation or maintenance of their rule.

FAITH AND CULTURE

One of the most complex problems with which we have to deal is the relationship between the Church, Christian faith, Christian thought, on the one hand, and the world's cultures on the other. Must Christianity jealously preserve its independence, guarding itself from all compromise or infiltration by the cultural environment which menaces it? If cultural syncretism is ruled out, how can both the purity of the faith and the reality of its presence and work in the world be maintained? This problem is now being given serious attention in many different places. I do not intend to describe the results here. I would only underline the increasingly political dimension of culture. The political ideologies penetrate the realm of culture, laying claim to a total explanation of history and human existence, and requiring total dedication by all men in all the aspects of their lives. Today the political controversies betray a ruthlessness and violence which had been absent from the scene of history for a long time. This is because, as political systems and cultural values overlap, political conflict becomes religious conflict. Thus communism declares itself to be criterion and source of truth in science, literature, and the arts as well as in political, social, and economic matters. In many parts of Asia and Africa today only a thin veneer of Western culture prevents complete integration of political, cultural, and social life within Hinduism, Islam, or Buddhism. And the American tendency to sanctify the American way of life and the witch hunt against those engaged in "un-American activities" extends considerably beyond the limits of politics into cultural and even religious areas.

I shall discuss two classical examples of this servitude or captivity of the church: the colonial liability weighing on the modern missionary movement and the progressively limited, middle-class character of the churches in Europe.

MISSION AND COLONIALISM

When we speak about the Protestant missionary movement of the last two centuries, we must recognize the tremendous work which was accomplished and be thankful to God. Nevertheless, as promising and fruitful as this tremendous renewal has been, we must frankly recognize its ambiguities. It was unfortunate, to say the least, that this great missionary effort coincided chronologically with the colonial expansion of Europe, which more recently is being replaced by the economic expansion and political domination of the United States. The interest of Western churches in Asian and African peoples grew naturally from the very moment their colonial conquest precipitated them into relationship with the West. What is more, the churches in the West quite rightly thought that the contacts established by this conquest between the colonized peoples and the Western nations offered a new opportunity, imposed a responsibility on the Western churches for evangelization. In the sixteenth century Spain and Portugal had reacted similarly at the time of the first wave of European expansion beyond the oceans; from the very beginning Catholic missionaries accompanied the *conquistadores*.

It remains, however, a deplorable fact that the European churches in the nineteenth century failed to realize that such a simultaneous movement of colonization and evangelization was bound in the long run to provoke serious difficulties. Doubts were raised about the integrity of the Christian missionaries, who were inevitably suspected of being the hypocritical agents of political domination, especially since the European churches, motivated by considerations of international convenience, divided up the map into mission fields following the political divisions their countries were negotiating at the same time. The French churches looked upon the French colonies in Africa as their mission fields; the British churches did likewise in India. This provided a situation ready-made to arouse the suspicion of political intentions hidden behind the missionary effort, all the more so, alas, since some missionaries—they were a minority, to be sure—sometimes did agree to serve as agents of their governments in the competition between rival world powers. Even when discounting these scandalous, though exceptional, instances, European missions "to the heathen" were very slow to distinguish between their calling to Christian witness and their civilizing function. They thus appeared to the Asian and African *élite* like cultural, if not political instruments of Western imperialism.

It is important to size up the situation in which the missionaries found themselves, and the reactions which were inevitably provoked by their activities. In the nineteenth century, and sometimes even today, Western missions had to face religious adversaries—Islam, Hinduism, Buddhism, primitive animism—as well as social disorder, economic misery, and a cultural vacuum. All of these constituted obstacles to evangelization and at the same time presented practical tasks for Christian love. For the missionaries to remain indifferent to such conditions would have been the worst denial of their preaching of the gospel. "It is not enough to say, 'Lord, Lord. . . .'" Under these circumstances the Christian missions had to establish far-reaching social and cultural programs. In doing this, what could they use, if not the Western heritage with which they were familiar? In the field of education, for instance, missionary schools and universities in most cases simply transplanted to Asia and Africa the methods, sometimes even the content, of Western teaching. The intention was excellent. But the result was that in the eyes of the non-Christian populations the missionary enterprise somehow looked like an appendage to the civilizing enterprise of Western powers. On the other hand the proclamation of the gospel itself and the building up of "younger churches" helped to burst the traditional structures of these Asian and African societies—and this is an inevitable development, as we shall see later. This all meant that the day a nationalist reaction set in, it was bound to attack the church as it struck out at Western political domination.

THE "YOUNGER CHURCHES" AND MODERN NATIONALISM

Even today the "younger churches" bear the marks of this cultural transposition of Western forms, methods, and values. Quite apart from such projects as schools, hospitals, etc., the life of the church itself often has a strangely Western character. Western visitors cannot help being amazed when they discover chapels in pseudo-gothic architecture on the shores of the Indian Ocean or the China Sea and hear singing of hymns whose music often recalls the worst period of Western hymnology; or when they find there the very same patterns of worship as in America, England, or France. But this is not all. While the majority of these churches move toward administrative independence and are no longer under the official direction of a foreign clergy, they nevertheless continue to send their best young pastors and theological students abroad, to Europe or America, to get the intellectual and practical education which is thought indispensable. Lastly these "young churches" still suffer from a terrible dependence for financial assistance on foreign countries—and all too often these are the former colonial powers—thus giving the impression of being branches of their mother-churches in Europe or America. Even though these links seem natural to the members of the churches, they are considered a threat to national independence and a hangover from colonial times by the non-Christian masses, and especially by the political leaders. In public opinion Christianity is nothing more than an aspect of the Western cultural inheritance.

It is therefore not at all surprising that in the twentieth century the majority of the great nationalist movements in Asia and Africa have taken an anti-Christian turn from the start. Even in its moderate form as with Gandhi in India, for instance, this nationalist reaction considers Christianity to be dangerous. Its spiritual riches are readily recognized, and Jesus is honored as one of the divine incarnations of Hinduism; but a faith which confesses Jesus Christ to be the only God and Saviour, and a Church which dares to bear witness to this assurance are forcefully rejected. The much more violent and radical nationalism of the Communist revolution in China has accused the Christian churches far more aggressively. The Chinese churches themselves have in recent years taken a stand against foreign missions that comes close to xenophobia or ecclesiastical nationalism. The so-called "three-self movement" harshly insists upon the urgent necessity of the Chinese churches to live on their own without any dependency whatever on the outside world, and to be solely responsible for the evangelization of China. The official declarations are clear enough: for the time being at least there is no place for foreign missionaries in China. This calls in question the universal and ecumenical character of the mission of the church, for this mission is universal not only because its scope is the world, but because its fulfillment is the common responsibility and hence should be the common venture for the whole Church of Jesus Christ, without distinction of national competence. Christians in the West for the most part have severely attacked the new Chinese missionary policy. I do not want to get into a detailed analysis of the situation. Nevertheless, I want to quote some recent conversations with Chinese friends which helped me better to understand their predicament and their efforts. Chinese Christians and foreign missionaries have often noted how Christianity, planted in China in the nineteenth century under the protection of Western canons, from the opium war in 1840 to the Communist revolution in 1949, has been closely dependent on Western Christianity. This dependency was intellectual and financial and the number of foreign missionaries was out of proportion to the Chinese clergy. The establishment of the Communist regime and the subsequent rupture of relations between China and the West was for the Chinese Christians like a brutal awakening from a long sleep, from a long illusion, to the hour of truth. Cut off from the churches in the West, they discovered that they were utterly without resources and found to their bewilderment that they were nothing but a foreign body in the midst of their own Chinese people. This rude awakening first of all compelled the Chinese churches to return to essentials, and all available information at the present time emphasizes the profound renewal of biblical faith. The churches had also to undertake a general reorganization, to reduce their administrative and institutional machinery to the measure of their own material and spiritual strength, and to launch a systematic effort to unify the many denominations imported from the West. Lastly, they have come to the conclusion that it is better, at least for some years to come, to renounce any appeal to outside support in the form of money or personnel. A young Chinese friend in speaking to me of this said, "Our churches are in the same situation as a country whose economy has been ruined by war. During the period of reconstruction, stiff tariff barriers are absolutely indispensable for the development of a national agriculture and industry. Foreign importation would otherwise ruin economic rehabilitaton. Likewise it is necessary that our Chinese churches, which are trying hard to take root among the Chinese people and to cleanse Christianity of all marks of foreign importation, for the time being shut themselves off from any dependency on or even any assistance from churches in other lands. Once firmly rooted, the church in China will be able to be open again to the outside world, to resume with its sister churches the co-operation necessary for the carrying out of the missionary task which is by nature ecumenical."

For the same reason young Christians in Asian and African countries which are struggling to achieve national independence identify themselves with their country's strife and take an active part in it which is almost out of proportion to the numerical strength of the small Christian minorities. For them it is an occasion to assert and to prove that Christian faith does not imply betrayal of one's country, that one can be both Christian and truly patriotic. Thus it is that Christians took part in the political struggle against foreign domination in India and Indonesia; thus in China, Christians approved of their country's intervention in Korea. Elsewhere and under different circumstances they have involved themselves in cultural or economic reconstruction, in public education, in fighting illiteracy, in medical services, and in the study of the problems of national reconstruction.

DIFFICULTIES OF INDIGENIZATION

The church can indeed be grateful that the ambiguities which marked the missionary movement in the nineteenth century have provoked these often violently nationalistic reactions. For their very violence has helped the church to become aware of the danger which was threatening it, and to take corrective steps. The problem, however, is far from solved. Many Asian churches have themselves fallen into the heresy of a thoroughgoing nationalism, making foreign missions scapegoats for their own unfaithfulness. Western churches also have often refused to open their eyes to their own unfaithfulness and have found their scapegoats in communism or Islam. Many difficulties persist. Think for a moment of the problem of developing an indigenous Christian theology and literature that would not reflect too exclusively the cultural influence of the West. The churches in

Asia are extremely cautious in this respect, much more so, very often, than some of the Western missionaries, who are eager to move ahead more rapidly. For to speak of indigenization on the intellectual level inevitably raises the serious danger of syncretism. Particularly in India, where the Hindu tradition represents after all the most perfect form of religious syncretism, the church must be on guard; the search for authentic cultural expressions all too easily slips into integration with the faith of all the pagan doctrines.

We should also keep in mind how difficult it is for these "younger churches" to let go of an ecclesiastical heritage, which is both rich and burdensome. When a Christian hospital has borne much fruit during a whole century, or when a missionary university has trained twenty generations of students, it is hard to give it up. Why discard an instrument that has proved to be so useful, and what should be done with all the buildings that are owned by the church? And yet these institutions have largely been responsible for the reputation of the "younger churches" as branch agencies of Western institutions. Beset by material difficulties as these churches are, it is difficult indeed to refuse financial assistance, generously offered by the churches in the West without any hidden intent of political or ecclesiastical domination, quite simply in the spirit of Christian fellowship. And yet to leave themselves vulnerable in any way to the accusation of financial dependence on the West is dangerous for these young churches and for their evangelistic outreach, not to mention the grave spiritual danger inherent in financial assistance out of proportion to their own resources. Finally, there is the complex problem of the proper balance between the urgent need for indigenization, for the young churches to take root within the nation and the culture where God has placed them, and their membership in a Church whose unity transcends all national divisions and all cultural differences.

THE CHURCHES AND ESTABLISHED ORDER

I come to my second example of the imprisonment of the church in the world. It is the bondage of the European churches to the limitations of the bourgeois (middle-class) character. This sad story begins, as has so often been noted, with the great Constantinian revolution, when an alliance was signed between the church, society, and the state. It is not important here to decide whether the church was right or wrong in accepting the transformation of the Roman Empire into a Christian empire; or whether in the Middle Ages the church could have separated itself more distinctly from the political, social, and cultural order. What is important is to understand the interlocking historical and theological developments that have led to the present situation.

Protestants are often inclined to put the blame for the ambiguous Constantinian alliance exclusively on Roman Catholicism. As a matter of fact, the sixteenth-century Reformation seems never to have seriously considered breaking it. The principle of *"cuius regio, eius religio"* (he who rules determines the religion) was followed in Protestant as well as Roman Catholic countries. Until the eighteenth century, religious tolerance was practically unknown. Only confessional minorities seriously tried to formulate principles of religious tolerance. Lutheran practice in Germany and Scandinavia, as well as the Geneva theocracy, assumed an identification of society and the church. Everywhere the state made itself the defender of the ecclesiastical monopoly and the church agreed to defend the political and social order and indeed civilization as a whole, which was willingly hailed as Christian. The symbiosis was complete.

It is against this alliance that revolt has exploded from the eighteenth century on. "Crush the infamy" is Voltaire's battle cry against a church that had become synonymous with the existing social order. Even the French revolutionary turmoil failed to break this tradition. Except for a few short episodes during the Terror, the climate of the French Revolution was clearly Constantinian. In 1791 the Civil Constitution for the clergy imposed by the revolutionaries on the Roman Catholic Church, far from breaking the bonds between church and society, tended on the contrary to reinforce them. Even at the time of the Terror, Robespierre reacted against the attempt at dechristianization and sought the official establishment of the worship of the Supreme Being, a modernized version of the same old alliance between church, state, and society. Finally the Concordat signed by Napoleon in 1801 marked an official renewal of the alliance. Other European countries, less profoundly shaken by the Revolution, had all the more reason to continue in the same way.

The early nineteenth century went even further, trying to make this alliance the explicit foundation of social and international order. The "Holy Alliance" signed by the sovereign powers was both reactionary and mystical. Throughout the century there was talk of the alliance between "throne and altar." The church identified itself with the struggle against all forms of subversion or even of political, social, or economic reform. In France it was the Roman Catholic Church which expressed itself most clearly, acclaiming in the monarchy a divine order and in bourgeois society the marks of a Christian civilization. It was not until the beginning of the twentieth century that Catholic voices timidly protested against this political syncretism. Protestantism was equally slow in disentangling itself from this political and social conformism. It was a Protestant, Guizot, who, before the horrifying misery brought about by the industrial revolution, offered as the only remedy to workers dying of hunger this slogan, supreme example of thoughtlessness or cynicism, "Get rich!"

Only at the end of the last century and in the first half of the twentieth century did the break between society and Christianity occur. The political parties of the left had come to power and brought about for their own benefit the disintegration of the Constantinian alliance, particularly in those countries under direct French influence. But strangely enough, the churches, and especially the Roman Catholic Church, tried to cling to the order of the past and to re-establish the alliance which the state had broken unilaterally. For several decades the political history of France was poisoned by the refusal of the Catholic church to accept the secularization of the state and of society which had become law with the Act of Separation of 1905. From 1940 to 1944 the Vichy regime, seen in this particular perspective, was nothing but a rebound of the outdated "Constantinianism" of bourgeois society, Catholic as well as Protestant.

Along with this involvement with the established social order, the churches made common cause with modern nationalism. The Reformation did not invent the national churches; they had existed since the thirteenth century at least. It is true that the unity of the Roman church acted as a brake on these nationalistic tendencies. The explosion of Western Christianity in the sixteenth century destroyed this brake. In accepting the principle of organizing themselves and functioning on a national basis, that is, within a framework taken over from the political entities, the Protestant churches contributed to the progress of European nationalism. Together with the Roman Catholic Church, they gave their unqualified blessing to any and all national causes. It required the disaster of the First World

War to arouse a reaction of protest against this consecration of the nation and its interests, against the scandal of the blessings of guns or of prayers against the enemy.

As might be expected, in accepting such bonds most of the churches also adopted what may be called a bourgeois way of life, at least since the bourgeoisie have dominated society in the nineteenth century. This bourgeois way of life appears for example in the tendency toward institutionalism, toward bureaucracy in church life so frequent still today among most of the majority churches or state churches. The idea itself of a salaried clergy implies that priests and pastors live a kind of bourgeois life and receive as preparation for their ministry the classical education so dear to the bourgeoisie. For a long time the European churches have been too willingly satisfied with reaching only the rural communities and the middle classes. Consequently Christian thinking about social and political matters remained conservative all during the nineteenth century, shunning the criticism of social institutions and structures, and proposing only individual charity as the remedy for injustice. Finally, since the establishment of the Communist regime in Russia, the churches or at least the majority of their members are easily caught up in the idea of an anti-Communist crusade, which is simply a new version of the Holy Alliance against all revolutions, and the result of the conviction that Christianity and the social order are bound in common cause.

The churches, having chosen to identify themselves in the past with one way of life and its particular political and economic order, now are imprisoned in it. They are alienating themselves from the ways of life and the political and economic orders that today are beginning to emerge. Their bourgeois character is the main cause of the churches' isolation in a time marked by the development of mass-societies.

SOME OTHER ILLUSTRATIONS

I described at some length these two classic examples of the imprisonment of the churches in the world. But there are many others. I shall mention only a few. There is the enslavement to racial prejudices, which reduces the church to pattern the structure and the life of the local congregations according to the prevailing discrimination or segregation of the environment. There is the cultural enslavement in the United States, where, as I have already pointed out, American culture, "the American way of life," is endowed with a strangely religious character.

I shall cite also, of course, the bondage which many churches in Communist countries accept. My critical remarks about the churches of the West are not meant to be a political critique of Western regimes and systems. What I think is dangerous in the growing middle-class mentality of European churches or in the ambiguities of the missionary enterprise in the nineteenth century are not the political consequences, but rather the results this situation may have for the churches and their ministry of evangelization. My verdict is therefore equally severe on those who choose to identify themselves with revolutionary social order, Communist for instance, or with a nationalist ideology such as today inspires certain Asian countries. There can be a conformity to the revolution just as well as a conformity to the established order, a Marxist conformity as well as a bourgeois conformity, a conformity of Bandoeng as well as a conformity of the Kremlin or of Washington. If this conformity is found less frequently in our Western world, it nevertheless exists and is for the church a temptation just as serious as any others.

I have tried to show how the churches can allow themselves to become enslaved by political, social, and cultural forces. How is this enslavement an obstacle to evangelization? In two ways, it seems to me. First, it helps to isolate the church, to shut it up in a kind of ghetto from which it cannot break out. Second, it perverts the Christian faith itself.

III. THE ISOLATION OF THE CHURCH

One serious consequence of the enslavement of the church to society is its isolation. When the church identifies itself too closely with a particular political order, it is in danger of losing contact with those groups which are in rebellion against that order; when it gives its blessing to one form of civilization, it frequently becomes blind to the emergence of new forms and loses its evangelistic thrust. It gradually becomes anachronistic, concerned exclusively with dead forms of society and culture, and ignoring the important events of the time.

THE CHURCH AND THE WORKING CLASSES

Once again I shall take an example from Europe and in particular from my own country, France. Much has been said in recent years about the industrial working class and the problems which it presents for missionary work. Studies have perhaps been overly preoccupied with statistics showing the advanced degree of dechristianization of the working class without sufficiently analyzing the cause of this. Working people in the large industrial centers of France are almost totally alienated from all Christian life and all church influence. This has been well enough known from a widely read book with the significant title: "France, Mission Field." It is however important to emphasize a very simple fact: if the French working class is not Christian today, it is because it has never been evangelized. If there ever was a dechristianization, it was dechristianization within the church itself, for a church which ceases to evangelize ceases to be Christian. It is significant that until recently there were almost no church buildings to be seen in the great industrial suburbs which sprang up in the nineteenth century. Our churches seem to have gone through the great industrial revolution, which transformed the face of Europe in the last century, in a state of deep intellectual torpor, without taking account of the sociological consequences of this technological earthquake, without noticing the abrupt appearance of a new social class of industrial workers, without troubling to set up the administrative and institutional machinery necessary to any evangelistic and preaching mission, and above all, without under-standing the new missionary problems raised by this sociological revolution.

During the last twenty years all the churches have made serious efforts to tackle these problems by examining the theological as well as practical aspects of their task among working class people. They experimented systematically with wholly new methods in order to be able, at the first opportunity, to launch a missionary program of great scope. These efforts met with considerable resistance. To mention only the most recurrent, many churches balk at the prospect of transferring the bulk of their resources in men and money from the depopulated rural areas to the great urban centers. The churches give the impression of fearing to be transplanted into an unknown world.

The churches also find it hard to accept methods of evangelization and forms of church life which, less foreign to the working class, shock the traditionalism surrounding ecclesiastical matters. Certain problems which evangelization has had to face during the last twenty years, without solving them satisfactorily, should be mentioned here. A strange phenomenon indeed was observed in the industrial outskirts of Paris as a result of the first systematic efforts at evangelization. On the one hand the rare workers who were converted most often left their factory jobs after a few months, becoming clerks or tradesmen, or lower middle class, at any rate abandoning their condition and their way of life as working-class people. On the other hand some of the converts, particularly those who had been reached through the ministry of the worker-priests, tried sincerely to enter into the life of a local congregation, only to give up very quickly and take refuge in their own working-class communities, so foreign to the normal structures of the church. A worker-priest told me some years ago how one of these men, who had tried very hard to become integrated in the life of the parish, came to him and said, "For me it's like this, see. Now I've got to choose. It's either believe in Jesus Christ or belong to the church." I am aware of the danger of generalizing lessons drawn from such experiments. Yet it seems that the major obstacle to evangelism among the working classes is the deep gulf that has been dug between the church and the working class in the course of over a century. Because social and political trends more and more separated the working class from the other sectors of society, the working people developed their own culture and their own forms of community life. As stated above, the church itself, chained to its middle-class values, is now totally estranged from the working classes and unable to speak their language or to offer them a home. The isolation of the official churches is such that experiments are being tried on the local level in forming strictly working-class Christian communities alongside the traditional parishes, and serious attention is being given to the possibilities of renewal inherent in these attempts.

THE CLERGY AND SOCIETY

If the church is isolated, what shall we say of the clergy? In Western societies, and probably in many others, mounting barriers separate it from the people to whom it desires to bring the Christian message. I already mentioned the bourgeois nature of the idea of a salaried clergy. It is impossible to overestimate how detrimental to evangelism is the practice of employing salaried clergy. I meet so many young pastors and missionaries who all repeat with bitterness and sometimes despair: "People refuse to listen to us or to believe us because they know that we are paid to preach." (Let us note in passing that salaried clergy did not appear until a few centuries after Christ, at about the same time as the Constantinian alliance between church and society.) We can therefore understand why today so many efforts are being made, especially by the younger clergy, to break away from the professional ministry and to find new patterns, such as a combination of pastoral or evangelistic work with some secular occupation.

Their protests as well as their projects of reform are based on a very simple discovery: to the very extent that a pastor is employed full-time and paid by the church, he finds himself cut off and isolated from other men, especially from those among whom he seeks to preach the gospel. Even the faithful sometimes consider their pastor as lazy, because he does not work as they do. He finds it increasingly difficult to reach out to the people whose way of life he does not share, whose psychological reactions, everyday problems, and political hopes he does not know. Various attempts are being made to overcome these barriers: a semester or more in factories or on farms for theological students; half-time ministry of certain pastors who become farmers, mechanics, or teachers; experiments of the worker-pastors. The worker-priests have been much talked about during the past few years, more, incidentally, with regard to the political implications than to the nature of their ministry. What the worker-priests—and the less well known worker-pastors—tried to do was to break through the isolation of the church by entrusting to the workers themselves the witness among their fellow workers. The problem is almost identical with that mentioned in connection with "younger churches" in Asia and Africa. Here also the church must be delivered from the liability of "foreignness," must proceed to some form of indigenization, or rather, in this case, of identification between the evangelist and those among whom he works. The political difficulties that provisionally ended the experiment of the worker-priests arose precisely from this concern for identification. Could the worker-priests be truly workers as long as they avoided that essential form of working-class life represented by trade-unionism, even if it was Communist dominated? I am certainly unable to answer this question. But it is impossible simply to leave the matter there. The problem is posed. Will the church have the courage to go as far as is necessary and as it can without compromising its faith and its witness, along the way of identification of the missionary with those to whom he goes?

All these experiments aim to "indigenize" the clergy, to overcome the most obvious forms of differentiation between clergy and ordinary men and women. The much debated question of the ordination of women should also be considered in this perspective: is there not real evangelistic significance in dispelling the idea that men alone qualify for the ministry? Of course, this is not the only, or even the primary argument, but no serious reflection about the place of women in the church can neglect it.

Have all these efforts by the clergy to identify themselves with society succeeded? We must not be unduly impressed by the apparent failure of the worker-priest movement in the French Roman Catholic Church. The condemnation of the Vatican was indeed limited to one form of this effort. It may be that such identification is impossible, or at least very difficult, within the Roman Catholic conception of the priesthood, and perhaps also contradictory to the idea of the Christianization of the world which characterizes Roman Catholicism. But many similar efforts continue in the non-Roman communions, and even in the Roman Catholic Church attempts are still being made to break down some of the walls of partition between clergy and society. The emphasis put everywhere on the ministry of the laity and particularly on its evangelistic ministry is a hopeful sign of an approaching change in the relationship, or lack of relationship, between church and society.

THE DANGERS OF IDENTIFICATION

The church's isolation in the midst of an indifferent world brings us back to the problem of the church's enslavement to certain forms of social and cultural life or certain political structures and conceptions. The origin of this enslavement should be noted. The church succeeded all too well in its effort to become indigenous, but that was centuries back, and by now it is all settled and quite at home. In accepting the Constantinian alliance in the fourth century, the church was seeking to fulfill its mission in the Mediterranean world of that time. The error, if there was one, consisted in accepting the support of political forces in fulfillment of this mission and in granting in exchange the church's spiritual and cultural support to the state and Roman society. It is certainly important for the church to identify itself with those to whom it is to proclaim the gospel. Yet the experience of history should teach us to show more wisdom. While the church must be truly present in the world, it must never become a tool of the world. It must never be tied to any institution or culture to the exclusion of others whose emergence is perhaps already being prepared in the interaction of historical forces.

EVANGELIZATION AND CHRISTIANIZATION

History can also show us the danger of another error; that of a progressive degradation of evangelization into a program of Christianization of the world. Evangelism does call for political, social, and cultural action. But the primary focus of evangelization remains the preaching of the gospel and the call to conversion, both of which are addressed to persons, both of which demand a personal response. Insofar as we are able to discern the fruits of evangelization—but let us always remember that finally God alone can judge—these fruits are the faith with which people receive and respond to the good news of Jesus Christ. This is to say that the ministry of evangelization is first of all directed to persons. Indispensable as is our responsibility toward political institutions, social structures, and cultural forms, it nevertheless has only a secondary and not a primary role in evangelization. Yet often in the past the churches seem, in fact if not in theory, to have considered the Christianizing of these institutions, structures, and forms as being the same thing as the evangelizing of persons. This equation, still current today, seems to me to present two serious dangers. From the practical point of view, any establishment of a "Christian" social order would be extremely fragile if it were not based in the faith of the members of this society. At a deeper level such a "Christianization" presupposes a certain syncretism. We cannot call human forms and institutions "Christian" without endowing them with a sort of sanctity, thus implying a logical continuity between revelation and human values. We then add something to revelation, as all syncretism does, and draw upon us the judgment of the gospel: "No one can serve two masters; for either he will hate the one and love the other, or he will be devoted to the one and despise the other" (Matt. 6:24). History has shown that whenever the church abandons itself to this Christianizing of human institutions and cultures, it becomes their prisoner. It ends up by being reduced to nothing more than the religious expression of a social order or of a particular civilization. In trying to Christianize the world, the church only secularizes itself, dechristianizes itself, loses the sense of its mission, ceases to evangelize.

If the church today wishes to break out of its isolation, it must first of all separate itself from all human institutions, whether political or cultural, whether representing the past or the future. Only by "demythologizing" all these human realities, by pointing out their human and relative characters, by withdrawing from them all attributions of sanctity can the church be actively present in the world and identify itself with the world in an effort, not to Christianize, but to evangelize.

THE TEMPTATION OF THE EASY WAY OUT

In such an effort of disinvolvement from the world, the church must also resist the temptation of taking the easy way out; for example, to undertake no missionary work except among those with whom the church feels at home, mainly in rural areas among middle-class people, instead of tackling the much more arduous task of evangelism among those to whom the church is foreign. The special situation of the intellectuals is instructive here. Fifty years ago they were a group almost impermeable, even hostile, to the Christian message. The church met with nothing but sarcasm or indifference from them. Things have changed a great deal. It remains true that the great majority of the intellectuals are still outside the church. They nevertheless pay a flattering attention to Christianity (perhaps too flattering for our humility). The great philosophical systems—rational positivism, scientism, historical humanism—having led not to progress, but to disaster, the intellectual climate is favorable to existentialism. Anything religious has become interesting. At the same time the theological renewal, revitalizing Christian thinking, has opened the way to a much more positive and fruitful confrontation between the church and the intellectuals than has been the case since the eighteenth century.

The church thus begins to find itself more at home among the intellectuals. Many Christians occupy prominent positions in intellectual circles. And, more and more, evangelizing the intellectuals has become a common concern. Again we follow the inclination for an easy way out. I can speak with conviction of this for I am professionally responsible for this task among intellectuals. Almost every day I see instances of how much more the church—much more so than at the beginning of this century—is interested in intellectuals than in other, less congenial, social classes.

Nobody thinks, I trust, that I am denying the importance of the task of evangelization among intellectuals. I know all to well both the richness and the difficulties. I know the urgency of it and I have often stressed its strategic importance. Yet at the same time I would like to point to the limits of this importance. It would be foolish to think that the intellectuals, in the classical understanding of the term, continue to occupy the same prominent place in the world they held fifty years ago. Their influence is declining. New social groups have succeeded them, the technicians in particular. The rise of totalitarianism also works against them. The intellectuals are distrusted, they are kept off to one side, at best they are tolerated. But they are no longer at the center of political strife or at the source of great historical movements. They are relegated to the role of spectators, extras, or, at best, the old men.

The church must continue its evangelistic work among the intellectuals, but it must also have the courage to penetrate those new cell groupings so essential to economic and social life today: the technicians, the managerial class in business and politics, and the industrial workers.

EVANGELISM AND "REVIVAL"

The same preference for the easy way out is found in the mass evangelism which has become fashionable again in our day, and of which Billy Graham is one of the better specialists. I want to analyze here neither the methods of mass meetings nor the message of the "evangelists" themselves, although a great deal could be said about the consistently apolitical character of some of these campaigns. What I want to stress is the fact that these "evangelists" are really more intent on awakening the Christians who have fallen asleep than on reaching the world outside the church. Billy Graham is the first one to admit that his message speaks primarily to those who, Christians at one time of their lives, have gradually slipped into indifference or unbelief. I do not suggest that these campaigns for "revival" are not useful. The preaching of the gospel, if it is faithful and effective, is always valid. The danger of the "revival" is that the church uses it as an alibi to excuse itself from the task of evangelization in really pagan circles. The danger of "revival" is that it gives a good conscience to a church which hasn't the courage to launch the assault on the non-Christian world.

THE ALIBI OF THE HOSTILE WORLD

This is, moreover, not the only alibi the church tries to find for itself. We are only too inclined to find the explanation of our indolence and failure in carrying out the mission of the Church in the opposition to us of the ideological forces of our time. We look for scapegoats as we analyze the modern religious or philosophical systems. We accuse Marxist materialism or nationalist fanaticism, the resurgence of ancient religions or the success of pseudo religions, astrology, spiritualism, magic. In short, it pleases us to believe that if the church does not evangelize, it is because the world is hostile to it and does not want the gospel. This is a historical error which is spiritually very dangerous. The world is hostile or simply not Christian: yes. But why should we be surprised? Jesus Christ declared this to us. Did he not warn us to be astonished and on our guard when the church and Christian faith become respectable? "Woe to you, when all men speak well of you, for so their fathers did to the false prophets" (Luke 6:26).

I am in no way implying that the study of the leading religions and ideologies of our time, and the analysis of the reasons for the hostility or indifference of men toward the gospel have not their usefulness. Such studies however should aim not at finding an alibi for our own shortcomings but at determining how we, as Christians, have fallen short of our calling. What is essential is to discover to what degree the indifference or hostility of the contemporary mind derives not from the stumbling block of the gospel—which cannot be lessened—but from all the stumbling blocks and offences of our unfaithfulness. For "woe to that man by whom the offence comes" (Matt. 18:7).

Our evangelistic task indeed demands this effort to understand the great currents of modern thought. How will we be able to speak to our contemporaries if we do not know their ways of thinking and their deepest convictions?

Of one thing I am certain: it is not in the world, but in the church itself that we must seek the origin and the cause of the present missionary crisis. The church alone is charged with the responsibility of preaching the gospel. It must proclaim it faithfully, yet leave it to God to bring forth his fruit. It is not we who convert men, but the Holy Spirit. At the same time the failure of our missionary efforts should ring in our ears like an alarm, compelling us seriously to ask ourselves: do we really lift up Jesus Christ before all men or are we unfaithful? What is the reason for the ineffectiveness of our missionary concern: man's wickedness or the church's wretchedness?

CHAPTER II

Theological Confusion, Politics, and Evangelism

I have tried to show that the church has allowed itself to become both enslaved by the world and isolated from it. We must now try to find out how this could happen, what theological route led to this historical deflection. To do this it is essential that we examine the Christian teaching about the relationships of the church with the world.

I. WITNESS AS DIALOGUE

The normal relationship between the Church and the world is that of dialogue. The whole New Testament underlines that we are not "of the world" but are sent "into the world" as ambassadors of a new and heavenly Kingdom. We are citizens of this Kingdom and therefore, while sent into the world, we are always strangers in it. The Church and its members are both independent from the world and responsible for it. It is their vocation to be, in the very midst of the world, an evidence of the presence of God. Christian witness consists in manifesting or making God known; in bringing to men the word of God; in continuing the work of Jesus Christ, the incarnate Word that has come among men. While it will never be on the same level as the incarnation which alone occurred once and for all, our human witness, if it is faithful, can reflect and in a sense continue it.

Christian witness must therefore always include two poles: God and the world. A witness, however correct theologically, if it does not really speak to people, if it does not strike home to men in the heart of their being, is unfaithful witness. In the same way, witness which is concerned only to be intelligible, to satisfy human needs, and does not seek before all else faithfully to reflect God's word, is not Christian witness either.

The church is always in danger of setting itself up as criterion, as the third pole of its own witness. The Church is certainly part of the Christian message: in proclaiming Jesus Christ, we proclaim his Body; in calling men to believe, we call them to become members of the Church. But the church must be very careful not to place itself on the same level with Jesus Christ. Its only significance is as a manifestation in the world of the love of our Lord. A church that proclaims, as an element of the gospel, its own institutional reality, its own achievements in history, perverts its whole message. This, incidentally, is one of the principal points over which the churches of the Reformation broke with Rome.

THE RETURN TO THE SOURCES

Evangelization therefore has these two poles: God and men. It proclaims Jesus Christ to the world. All Christian witness consequently should be based first of all in a return to the source of our knowledge of Jesus Christ. Study of the Bible and, along with that, the study of the doctrines of the Church, the practice of prayer, and the partaking of the sacraments are the essential conditions of evangelization. Experience incidentally has shown, as I have mentioned, that in times of crisis the renewal in the churches of their sense of mission always began with a return to essentials, with a deepening of their faith and their Christian life. I have spoken already of the Chinese churches in the period since the Communist revolution. Their first reaction was a systematic effort of Bible study and of theological reflection. They have rediscovered that the Christian life is blind dependence on Jesus Christ; but they refuse or declare themselves as yet unable to formulate this dependence into a doctrinal system or to give it any institutional or theological character. As one Chinese Christian has expressed it: "We see now clearly that the reason why we are Christians, once we have ruled out the many 'reasons' which we had considered decisive, was Someone. We are Christians because of Someone, Jesus Christ. . . . We then had to ask ourselves: Who is Jesus Christ? It is because of this question, repeated in ten thousand ways, that we found ourselves again and were strengthened, going from discovery to discovery, from wonder to wonder in ever more numerous Bible Study circles centered around the unceasing inquiry: 'Who is this Lord who sets us apart and sets us also in the midst of others?' Our congregations, our student and youth groups have thus vehemently 're-sourced' themselves and are now made up of Christians, sometimes fewer in number, but truly renewed and ready to make their witness."

CONCERN FOR PERSONS

This return to the sources, however, must be accompanied by a return to man. Are we profoundly concerned about those to whom we are sent to proclaim the gospel? Are we really interested in them and do we love them? I remember how some years ago a Finnish student was telling me how distressed she was by her inability to speak of Jesus Christ to one of her roommates. It became clear in the conversation that she was more anxious about her own faithfulness than about her friend. She did not really know her. She had never taken pains to show any human interest in her. She knew very little about her friend's family and was not concerned about her plans for the future, her hopes, and her fears. Her roommate was nothing but an *occasion* to announce Jesus Christ. In such circumstances witness is impossible. This is only an example of one of our most frequently recurring mistakes. We are unwilling to admit that we must be concerned not only about Jesus Christ and our faithfulness to him, but also about others and our faithfulness to them. We find again here on this level the duality and the profound unity of the summary of the Law. We cannot love God without loving our neighbor. We cannot love our neighbor without sharing with him the joy of the gospel, nor can we share this with him if we do not love him. Our witness consists also in finding how to love those who do not share our faith, but to whom we would like to make it known. Witness is the point at which the two commandments meet.

To be concerned about others, nevertheless, is not enough. Human sympathy is indispensable, but not sufficient. Let us not forget that the Greek word "sympathy" implies participation, the sharing in suffering or joy. Christian witness requires us at all times to try genuinely to enter into the human experiences of those whom we seek to reach. By our testimony itself we compel others to face a new experience which challenges their very existence, the experience of the judgment of God, of repentance and conversion. The witness must know how to stand out of the way of the Lord to whom he witnesses, placing himself not as an obstacle between God and man, but placing himself before the Word of God along with the person to whom he speaks. The witness, spokesman for the eternal gospel of Jesus Christ, must be fully man, sharing the weaknesses and burdens of humanity, its hopes and enthusiasms. In other words, it is essential that the gospel be announced to men by their own kind, which is to say, in our day, by those who participate in the political longings and anxieties of the twentieth century.

Christian witness is a two-way traffic. Repentance and faith are always marked by an element of protest, of struggle with God, such as Jacob went through at the ford of the Jabbok before he became "Israel." As witnesses we are asked to accompany those to whom we declare the gospel along the whole way of this confrontation and contest; with them we must experience once again the struggle of faith. And how can we, if we escape into a proud indifference toward the world, with its wretchedness and horrors, but also with the grandeur given to it by the love whereby God encompasses it? Witness can therefore never be reduced simply to the proclamation of the gospel; it always requires that the witness also walk with the new believer on the hard and wonderful road from unbelief to joyful certainty.

KNOWING HOW TO LISTEN

The confrontation is not limited to the encounter with God, the struggle of faith. Witness is also struggle with the world. I do not want to talk about Christian apologetics here. I am very skeptical about its missionary value. I am thinking rather of the danger that menaces the church when it takes a purely negative attitude of judgment and condemnation toward the world, toward its expectations or its certainties. We are indeed the bearers of the gospel, but we have no monopoly on it. We remain "unprofitable servants." God can speak through unbelievers as well as through Christians, through history and nature as well as through the Church. True, there is no other criterion of revelation than Jesus Christ himself as witnessed to in holy scripture. But God can choose at any time to speak to us as he sees fit, often through the most disconcerting channels. Just think of those who got to know Jesus Christ thanks to war and its atrocities.

In any case, in our witness we must always be on the alert. This world with which we are in continuing conflict, with which we have joined battle, may suddenly transmit to us a word of God. We must learn to listen to the world as well as to speak to it, to be humble as well as sure of the gospel. Among adherents of a pagan religion or a modern ideology we all too easily affirm our own faith and condemn their convictions. Our faith is indeed true, but not because it is ours; it is true because it is Christ's. This does not mean that we have nothing to learn from human convictions. To take a painful example, just think of our humiliation as Christians before the complete devotion of the Communist to his convictions and his party, before his seriousness and his self-abnegation. Let us go one step further. When we see this Communist enthusiasm, this generous search for a better world, "for tomorrows that sing," can we then fail to discern behind the demonic perversions of ideology and party the word of condemnation which God pronounces upon us: "Why have you done nothing to relieve human misery? Why have you left to others to fight for a better tomorrow?" In other words Christian witness, the affirmation of the one Lord and one salvation, can never be mere rejection of the world; the church must confess its failures and learn from the pagan world. The church must listen to the world.

In brief, the church and those who witness for Jesus Christ must be willing to enter into a dialogue with the world; they must break away from the fatal monologue that threatens the self-satisfied church. It is clear there can be no compromise with a world in rebellion against God, no adulteration of the gospel by this or that human wisdom. Neither can there be any pride or scornful indifference toward this world which God loves and uses, when he so wills, to pronounce judgment on his church.

II. THE TEMPTATIONS OF PIETISM AND CATHOLICISM

The church today seems in danger of losing precisely this sense of dialogue. Two heresies, though diametrically opposed to each other, both reject any dialogue with the world. The church has been in danger of losing its sense of mission every time it has been threatened by one of these heresies, the pietist or the catholic. I realize the danger there is in using these terms which have theological as well as historical connotations. I would have preferred to describe the menace without calling it by name. I do not wish to insult anyone, nor to suggest that these two dangers imperil only those who declare themselves to be pietists or catholics. If I use these words it is only because pietism and catholicism offer to the church the best illustrations of the danger it must avoid.

PIETISM

I will call the "pietist temptation" that tendency, frequent among Protestants, to consider that the Christian life consists above all in preserving our faith, our moral life, free from the corrupting influences of the world, including naturally those of politics. For the pietist the world is evil; the Christian life requires separation from the world, a retreat into holiness apart from the world. Christian witness, therefore, must summon men to make the break and to escape from the world and its perils. Pietism rejects the world and digs a gulf between the Church and mankind; it condemns the world and remains indifferent to what is happening there.

Some will object to this description by pointing to the pietist missionary zeal. I do not deny this. At the present time a great many of our evangelists and missionaries come from pietistic circles. This should be for us good reason for repentance, but it does not prove anything about the value of pietism itself. What is paradoxical—I even venture to say non-Christian—in the pietist message is its demand that men forsake the world and its sin in order to know Jesus Christ, while the gospel proclaims that salvation is free and only the experience of it delivers us from sin and enslavement to the world. It is significant that the pietistic message has its greatest success among people who have experienced failure, discouragement, or despair and who no longer expect anything in this world. It finds little response among those who share the excitements and hopes of their day. For this reason pietism often engages in negative apologetic arguments aimed at undermining human convictions and hopes in order to prepare the ground for favorable reception of the gospel. As if Jesus Christ ever indulged in such demolition! As if the gospel,

in order to be believed, needed to be proved as the only solution!
As if the gospel were human wisdom, perhaps the most perfect
wisdom, but still on the same level as other human knowledge!

In any case, pietism has demonstrated beyond any doubt its fundamental indifference to politics, which it considers as one of the manifestations of sin. Pietist missions "in pagan lands" have always safely
kept the faithful from entanglement in political discussions and
activities. Is it necessary to suggest that this "apolitical" attitude is
equal to a very real political choice, that of conformity? To reject
politics is to support the *status quo.* Hence we should not be surprised to see pietist groups showered with the favors of governments
that are most hostile to the Church. I point out this situation
only to strengthen my thesis: pietism refuses any kind of dialogue
with the world and withdraws so far from it that there is no longer
any common interest, any real point of contact. The world is as
indifferent to pietism as pietism itself is to politics.

POLITICAL CATHOLICISM

At the opposite pole lurks the temptation of "political catholicism." I am dealing here not only with Roman Catholicism but
with an error which Protestants also frequently make. Whereas
pietism repudiates the world and escapes from it, catholicism—I
should perhaps speak of political and cultural catholicism—attempts
to absorb the world into the church, to accept as Christian its
political, moral, and aesthetic values. It thereby goes hand in hand
with a perversion already mentioned, that of substituting Christianization for evangelization. Political and cultural catholicism establishes two basic ontologically substantive realities. One of these
links together God, Jesus Christ, the Church, and theology; the
other includes the world, its culture and institutions, its values and
orders. Political catholicism then tries to integrate these two realities
within the framework of a church whose catholicity consists not
only in the unity of Christians of all times and in all places, but
also in the whole spectrum of secular values to which finally nothing
human is foreign. Catholicism thus becomes synonymous with
synthesis, syncretism, almost pantheism.

We have, unfortunately, only too many examples of this. The
Roman church, in particular, has made a specialty of it, "baptizing"
into the church remnants of pagan cults with their rites and super-

stitions; philosophical systems, from Aristotelianism to Bergsonism or existentialism; and above all, political and social concepts which concern us here even more directly. Today in the Roman church "integrism" is the form of this drive for assimilation. "Integrism" seeks to include in the official teachings of the church, along with the traditional theology, the political and social concepts, indeed the whole civilization, which the Roman church had sanctified in the Middle Ages. This would accord them final recognition as Christian. Thus there is a reactionary bias, a looking to the past, that characterizes political catholicism. But whenever a church consecrates or absorbs human values, it faces a similar problem. This is true today of those, both Protestants and Catholics, who call themselves "progressive Christians." Instead of utilizing the Thomist criterion of integrism, they endeavor to lay down Christian political and cultural norms in terms of twentieth-century ideologies. Both leftists and reactionaries deny any real discontinuity between God and the world. They make the Church a bridge which binds God and the world together. The Church thus becomes the Kingdom of God under construction, the beginning of the new creation within history.

Under these conditions, as in the case of pietism, the dialogue between the Church and the world becomes impossible. There can be no dialogue except between two who address each other. Two partners are needed for a dialogue. In this catholic perspective the Church and the world arrive at unity. The relationship of the Church to the world leads to the control, in completely secular ways, of the Church over the world or, should the latter resist such assimilation, to a crusade of the Church against the world. The Church becomes merely a human entity. In its attempt to Christianize the world, the Church only secularizes itself. Christianity is reduced to the role of one religion among many.

ESCHATOLOGICAL HOPE

These seem to me to be the two temptations to which the church is exposed. How can we resist them? The church must rethink the biblical conception of history and particularly of Christian hope, of eschatology, of "the last things."

Some brief outline must suffice here. Our hope is founded in this, that Jesus Christ has overcome the world and, by this victory, founded a Kingdom whose reality we already experience as we live by faith.

This Kingdom, still hidden, will one day be manifested in all its glory, and that day will be the end of history. No one knows when this event will take place, or how, but only that it will surely come. This hope is not founded on any optimism about the progress of the world, or any belief that it will gradually be transformed into the Kingdom. On the contrary, if the Bible makes any prediction it is rather one of the progressive deterioration of the world. "When the Son of Man comes, will he find faith on earth?" (Luke 18:7). Our hope is built on the one victory won by Jesus Christ and on the certainty of his glorious return. Of this Kingdom we know only one thing, that he is its king. What is our calling, our responsibility? To believe this good news and to proclaim it to all men, for it is meant for all: "For the Son of Man came to save the lost" (Matt. 18:11). To all we must bring the assurance that neither life nor death, nor principalities, nor powers, including political or economic determinism, will be able to separate us from the victorious love of Jesus Christ.

This victory, this expectation of the Kingdom, is the basis for our witness, for our dialogue with the world. To the world we bring the news of the coming Kingdom. In the world we see the reality which Christ has defeated, and also that to which the Kingdom is promised. Here and now we testify to this Kingdom that is coming by our words, our deeds, by our life in the Church; we are its prophets. Such witness, of course, inevitably determines our attitude toward politics.

This kingdom we proclaim is, however, not only to come. Though hidden, it is already real. The Christian is already a citizen of it, for "our life is hid with Christ in God" (Col. 3:3). This is why we must "set our minds on things that are above," "put off the old nature with its practices," live like those for whom "there can no longer be Greek and Jew . . . barbarian or Scythian, slave or free man," "put on . . . compassion, kindness, lowliness, meekness, and patience, forbearing one another, and, if one has a complaint against another, forgiving each other . . . ," work heartily, whatever our task, and treat one another "justly and fairly" (Col. 3:3 ff.). Our whole life in fact must show forth the reality of Christ's Kingdom, making it visible to the world through our obedience. Thus the Kingdom is for us just as much present as future. And this is so because it is also past. For it has been established once for all by the cross and the resurrection; it is future because we hope for it, and present, because we live in it.

The pietist and the catholic deviations seem to me to deform this doctrine of the Kingdom of God and its coming, this eschatological hope. Pietism emphasizes the catastrophic character of the final event which will terminate history and usher in Christ's Kingdom. Quite apart from the extravagance of the extremist sects, which claim to know the exact way and date of Christ's Second Coming, pietism projects this eschatological event entirely into the future. It is assigned an essential place, yet it remains within history, awaiting us somewhere along our earthly journey. It is a promise to the chosen few, and a menace to the world doomed to annihilation. Thus the apocalyptic event of the return of the Lord assumes its own significance, independent of the Lord himself. This explains why it can represent a terrifying threat instead of a wonderful promise. Certainly it is something very grave, something terribly serious to appear before God; but the Lord who at the end of time will come to judge all creatures is Jesus Christ, the Lord of the cross, whose formidable holiness is inseparable from the promise of his love. Eschatological hope is therefore not the dreadful anticipation of a cosmic catastrophe, but the joyful waiting for our Saviour. It is worthwhile to note what role the ultimate destruction of the lost world plays in pietism. I remember hearing a pietist say once that if he did not believe that hell would one day be filled with the damned, he could not believe in Jesus Christ. Whether we believe in hell and damnation or in universal salvation, can we find the source of our faith anywhere else than in the redeeming work of Jesus Christ? I only know that it is a frightful distortion of the gospel to make hell a condition of faith. We are to be concerned about ourselves and not about God's judgment on the world; this is exclusively his concern, and he loves the world. In any case it seems clear that the pietist attitude of indifference and fear, and its aversion to politics, are closely related to the conviction that the world is doomed to destruction, to damnation.

Political catholicism, on the other hand, while in theory it maintains the eschatological doctrine, ends up by forgetting the return of Christ. The coming of the Kingdom ceases to be the great event which the Church vigilantly and obediently awaits, because the Kingdom is a matter for historical realization, an affair of the Church. The Church, in gradually conquering the whole world, in absorbing it, becomes itself the Kingdom. The return of the Lord becomes unnecessary, since he is already on earth, present and visible in the Church. Eschatology is in the process of realization in history. For this reason Christian witness, the proclamation of the Kingdom, can take the form of efforts toward political and social domination, of Christianization of the world, of an extension of the Church. The Kingdom of Christ is transformed into an imminent historical phenomenon, and Christian hope is stifled by ecclesiastical will to power.

I am fully cognizant of the danger inherent in any such terse description of the pietist and the catholic distortions. It borders on caricature. But I do not wish here to go into a history of dogma. I have simply tried to discern the temptations that beset all of us so that we may better withstand them. The majority of pietists and catholics will refuse to be identified with the description I have given of pietism and catholicism. And rightly so, because there is more in their faith than the errors of which I have spoken. But this is beside the point. The church must avoid these two temptations, and in order to do so, must recover a solidly biblical interpretation of history and of the end of history. This is the only way for the church to rediscover why and how it must enter into dialogue with the world, and thus find again the meaning of evangelization and also of Christian responsibility in the political realm.

CHAPTER III

Theological Renewal and Political Thinking

I. ETHICS AND WITNESS

Let us reread Peter's speech in Jerusalem on the day of Pentecost. When the crowd asked him what they should do, he answered, "Repent, and each one of you be baptized in the name of Jesus Christ to obtain the forgiveness of your sins; and you shall receive *the gift of the Holy Spirit*. For the promise is to you and to your children and to all that are in far off countries, every one whom the Lord our God calls to him" (Acts 2:38–39). The witness of the primitive church invariably contains three essential elements: the good news of salvation, the call to repentance, and the new life in the Holy Spirit. In his letters Paul is always careful to relate logically his doctrinal exposition to his ethical conclusion. After the first eleven chapters of his letter to the Romans, where Paul gives a striking interpretation of salvation, follow five chapters of moral and political exhortation. He introduces them with this phrase: "I appeal to you *therefore*, brethren, in the name of divine compassion, to offer your bodies as a living sacrifice, holy and acceptable unto God, which is your reasonable service" (Rom. 12:1).

Must we, further, grant to the Church a place in our witness? The answer is both yes and no. The Church is part of the gospel. Yet it is not a separate element in our proclamation, added to the story of God's act in Jesus Christ and the ethical teachings deriving from it. On the contrary the Church shares in both elements at the same time. Because it is the Body of Christ, the Church is part of the good news. Because it is the place of our faithfulness, the community that believes, loves, and hopes, the Church is part of the ethical teaching, representing one of the forms of obedience to which God calls us. To introduce the Church as a third element would pervert our witness: the Church is not a fourth person of the Trinity.

Let us consider not only the objective content of our witness, but also its form, the ways of expressing it, to underline the difference between its doctrinal and ethical elements. The preaching of Jesus Christ and his reconciling and redeeming act retains a permanence which the ethical teaching cannot have. Jesus Christ accomplished the work of salvation once and for all. We have nothing to add to it, but only to find the language, the words and the concepts, the images that would help men understand the eternal gospel. We must not change one iota of it, but neither must we use a vocabulary that has been old for twenty centuries; or we might as well be speaking Greek or Hebrew.

By contrast, the preaching of repentance and of new life in the Spirit, in other words the Christian ethic, varies with the times, places, and circumstances. Christian ethics is simply the imitation of Jesus Christ, living according to the image of God, finding again the obedience of faith, our original nature which our sin had soiled and deformed. The Christian ethic may therefore be seen in two perspectives. First, as a judgment whereby God condemns our sin and all our particular sins, compelling us to repent. Second, as an exhortation to live according to the Spirit, in imitation of Christ. "Have this consciousness in you which was in Christ Jesus," or, in another translation, "Carry into your mutual relationships, that affection which you feel in fellowship with Christ Jesus" (Phil. 2:5).

For either of these perspectives the ethical teaching is to some extent conditioned by our historical and social environment. Ethics as judgment of sin, condemns our own disobedience in given situations, as well as all the political and social perversions of our time. Ethics as exhortation to live according to the Spirit, will outline how this spiritual life may thrust itself into a particular social and cultural context. Hence the ethical teaching of the Church cannot be the same in the medieval, feudal period and in our atomic age. The missionary in the African forest cannot hold out to primitive peoples living by hunting and fishing the same patterns for Christian life as he does to the industrial workers in Western Europe. Perhaps, moreover, the first generations of missionaries made mistakes here. For example, the question is being raised today as to whether the traditional doctrine of the church about marriage is right for countries which have always been polygamous, and whether the church did not transplant too hastily the Western Christian conception of the couple. Would it not be possible, without betraying the essentials of the gospel, to discover new forms of this human relationship that are better suited to sociological conditions so entirely different from those of Europe or America? It is also evident today that in the course of the last centuries the church has neglected to work out an ethic specifically related to professional questions and intended to help resolve some of the problems in modern trades and professions that present real difficulties for Christian obedience.

GOSPEL AND LAW

In the field of Christian ethics the theologians have sometimes tried to establish a distinction between the Old and the New Testament, describing the Decalogue as the divine guide of human society, and the Sermon on the Mount as the definition of the life of the Christian in the Church. This distinction seems to imply another, even more serious distinction between moral law and gospel which leads to the dangerous moralism which Paul so vigorously condemned. "You are no longer under the law but under grace" (Rom. 6:14). This is why we must no longer sin, and not because the law has any validity of its own apart from the gospel. "What then? Are we to sin because we are not under the law, but under grace? By no means!" (Rom. 6:15). It is the grace of Jesus Christ and faith in him that breaks the inevitability of sin, condemnation, and death. To re-establish the autonomy of the law alongside of the gospel would cancel out grace, place us again under condemnation, throw us back into the infernal cycle of guilt and merit. The opposite is true, and we must hold fast to it: grace is our law. Jesus Christ himself is the content of our ethic. Knowing him by faith we are set free by him to live as children of God.

Let us be careful to avoid the danger of keeping truth and salvation neatly separated on the one hand from ethics and morality, and from our individual and corporate responsibility on the other.

At the beginning of this chapter I pointed to three elements of
Christian witness: the proclamation of the gospel, repentance, and
new life. This distinction is useful only for clarification. If we follow
the biblical revelation, the preaching of the gospel and ethical teaching are one and the same thing. All ethical teaching in the Old
as well as in the New Testament proclaims to men the good news
of God's love. The Ten Commandments and the Sermon on the
Mount describe God's holiness, righteousness, and love and only
then give us moral instruction. Conversely, the preaching of the
cross and resurrection is the most stringent and urgent call to repentance and sanctification. It seems therefore mistaken to take the
Ten Commandments as a social ethic, and the Sermon on the Mount
as the formulation of the Christian life, first and foremost because
this differentiation implies a gulf between ethics and the doctrine
of salvation. These two texts, along with all others that deal with
moral or political questions in the Bible, proclaim above all the
good news of God's love; Christian ethics has to be derived from
this. We cannot know the content of the ethic of faith without first
passing through the experience of faith. Every attempt to apply
directly the ethical texts of the Bible without passing through the
medium of faith is bound to lead to a moralizing and legalistic
formalism, which is contrary to the gospel.

I have said that ethical teaching must vary according to time,
place, and circumstance. I must add that in no case should it be
reduced to casuistry, which enumerates all possible moral problems
and formulates solutions satisfactory to each. On the contrary, because obedience can only be the fruit of faith, Christian ethics will
consist in a quest in each particular circumstance to discover, in
faith and in the light of faith, what is our particular obedience,
the service to which God calls us. This is a task of the Church
and not of the individual Christian living in isolation. Together,
helping one another, we must learn how to repent of our wickedness
and that of the world in which we exist, and to live in imitation of
Jesus Christ.

ETHICS AND POLITICS

I want to lay stress on the political character of this ethical quest.
We must be sensitive to the political temptations which assail us
and, with us, all men of our times. We must be alert to the political

questions that engross them. People in the twentieth century live in
a political context that marks their entire existence. Their temptations and their sins are, to a large extent, political. Politics is a matter
of daily concern, the cause of the most intense devotion as well as
of the deepest disillusion.

What are these political temptations? Examples abound. The
temptation of power, of wealth, formerly simply individual, takes
on a more and more collective character: national egotism, the
struggle between social classes, political competition, conflict between
nations, cartels, and economic monopolies. Pride, the primary form
of sin, very often has the same kind of political character: pride of
race or pride of nation with their supporting procession of fears and
hatreds. Falsehood and deceit poison all political life: propaganda,
always intended to delude by hiding the truth or insinuating error,
is the favorite weapon of all political regimes, of all the parties and
special interest lobbies. Modern man bathes in deceit and is guilty
of it from the moment he agrees to live in society. Decent people,
of course, do not commit murder; but are we so sure that our hands
are clean? Do we not profit from an economic system which assures
us of abundance by starving others? We have not borne arms in an
unjust war, but our country has perhaps enriched itself through
bloodshed. The armament race shocks us, we condemn the recourse
to war, but our selfishness, our pride, our impassioned violence make
us co-responsible for international tensions. But most of all we
succumb to the worst temptation, indifference to human suffering
and to the sin which causes it, and this in a time when men are
largely victims of their political existence and its disorders.

Political questions are on everyone's mind. We are living through
a time when politics becomes religion. All political philosophies tend
toward totalitarianism, demanding loyalty without reserve from their
adherents. This is true for the explicitly totalitarian ideologies such
as communism, fascism, nationalism and also, in a more insidious
way, of liberalism, humanism, and individualism. All conflicts,
whether social or international, take on the character of religious
wars.

Men today seem to be launched on a desperate quest for a social
ethic. How shall we live in modern society? How can we teach men
to act justly, for the common good? How can we organize a society
which serves man instead of enslaving him? Our political climate is
curiously moralistic. The puritan aspect of communism has often

been noted; it practices self-examination not only in political matters but also in moral questions. All modern governments do all they can to find moral justification for their conflicts and no longer, as in the past, make a cynical display of their ambitions. Newspapers publish the magnificent declarations of all the parties on their ideals of justice, liberty, and honesty.

As a repercussion of all this moralizing, people in the twentieth century surrender to despair when they fail in their efforts to find a satisfying social ethic. They laugh, of course, at the great slogans, pompous and romantic, of the last century. "Liberty, equality, fraternity"—words, nothing but words. . . . It has become smart to be witty and play the cynical and disillusioned. But the youth of today, which repudiates the political and cultural heritage of former generations and shuts itself up in a silence often heavy with bitterness, is, perhaps without being really aware of it, searching for an ethic. Too uncertain to chart their own road, today's young people withdraw into a laborious individualism; they wait, without quite knowing what for. They are certainly awaiting masters who can do what their elders can no longer do: teach them how to live together, in peace, in justice, and in freedom. They are looking for an ethic of happiness, for a way of life which is collective as well as personal. This is a far cry from the amoralism of André Gide. The whole of modern life revolves around this hope, this search for a social ethic. Has the church anything to offer in response to this longing of modern man? Will it be able to define a social ethic, to seize this splendid opportunity to announce the good news to men, to help them to live in an increasingly complex, disconcerting, alien world, and to discover the one truth which, beyond all uncertainty, makes possible a life full of meaning because it has a hope?

II. MAIN LINES OF CHRISTIAN THINKING ABOUT POLITICS

In the preceding chapter I tried to describe the theological confusion in which the political thinking of the Church is submerged, and to point out some of the most damaging errors. I can now show more optimism. While the confusion still profoundly affects the Church, nevertheless, in the course of the last decades, the kind of progress was made which makes it possible to specify the foundations upon which a Christian socio-political ethic could be constructed.

THE REDISCOVERY OF POLITICS

The theological rediscovery of politics is largely the result of the accelerated rhythm of events since the beginning of the century. The succession, in chain reaction, of international conflicts, economic crises, social upheavals, and political revolutions compelled the church to reconsider the claims of its faith in response to this turmoil. This whole endeavor was, of course, not simply the result of the contemporary political chaos. Those engaged in it were careful to base their inquiry and their definitions on the only solid foundation, the biblical, and they carried out their work within the community of the Church, whose true meaning they rediscovered. It was, moreover, at the beginning of this century that the fuse was lit for the great theological renewal which is likely to assign to our time a place equal to that of the sixteenth century in the history of theology. Theological reflection and political analysis went hand in hand, enriching each other. While the doctrinal renewal gave to political thought a new understanding of the relevance of the Bible, of the Christocentric character of relevation, and of the living reality of the Church, the pressure of political events helped theologians to renounce their old humanistic illusions and forced them to return to the only truth which cannot be shaken by political or cultural disaster. For my generation it was providential that we had discovered Karl Barth's theology before the catastrophy of 1940. After the war, the German occupation, and the Resistance, our attitude toward political problems in 1944 showed us by comparison the somewhat naïve enthusiasm that had motivated us ten years earlier. I can only be thankful to God that he did not abandon us in the disaster but gave us the help of his Word.

When the collapse of France destroyed all the things in which we had believed—political, moral, and cultural—when we were compelled to revise all our values, it was a blessing that we could go back to the Bible, which we had already begun to learn to read. I wish to acknowledge our immense indebtedness and gratitude to Karl Barth, or rather for what he helped us to learn from the gospel and its political teaching. I am not suggesting that the church should undertake a sort of scholastic analysis of Barthian thought. What is needed above all in order to discover the Christian significance of politics is the experiment of political engagement. But the church should thank God that the great theologians of today are men who teach us again to plumb the depths of the scripture which guides us through the struggle of faith and of social responsibility.

I would like now to distinguish four essential themes which seem to stand out in all recent thinking by the church about politics. I do not mean that there are four different and contradictory conceptions of the Christian significance of politics. Rather, these are four complementary aspects, four definitions, each reflecting something of the total biblical base, four lines of thought which deserve, each one, our attention and, all together, enable us better to understand the nature of our responsibility.

THE ORDER OF GOD

God has instituted order in the political realm. This is the most commonly accepted basis for the Christian's political responsibility. From this perspective our task essentially is to maintain in the world an order in accordance with the will of God, obeying therefore the authorities to whom he has entrusted the administration of justice. As Paul says, "There is no authority except from God, and those that exist have been instituted by God. . . . Therefore one must be subject, not only to avoid God's wrath but also for the sake of conscience. . . . For the authorities are ministers of God, attending to this very thing. Pay all of them their dues . . ." (Rom. 13:1–7). Or as he says elsewhere, "I urge that supplications, prayers, intercessions, and thanksgivings be made for all men, for kings and all who are in high positions, that we may lead a quiet and peaceable life, godly and respectful in every way" (I Tim. 2:1–2).

There is nothing complicated about this. God wills that men should live decently, in peace and tranquillity, according to his commandments. It was with this intention that he created and redeemed us. But our sin has introduced into the world the seed of death, of disorder, of destruction; the wages of our wickedness should really be general annihilation. To prevent this God in his mercy has established authorities charged with maintaining, by force if necessary, a minimum of order, freedom, and justice. The Christian must be watchful that such order, without which existence would be impossible, be maintained. In New Testament days this political responsibility could be limited to obeying the emperor, magistrates, all the established authorities, and to praying for them also, of course. But we live in a completely different situation today. As citizens in liberal democracies, we ourselves exercise a part of this public authority, if only by our right to vote. We must therefore exercise this authority, knowing full well that we are responsible for maintaining an order of justice and freedom that God wants to see prevail. Failure to vote thus constitutes a characteristic unfaithfulness to the will of God. Voting in accordance merely with our political prejudices and our personal interests, without considering the social and international significance of our vote, is equally to trespass against the commandments of God.

What about Christian political responsibility under dictatorial regimes? Perhaps there the Christians have no other choice but to obey the authorities as long as their conscience permits them to do so. Yet even in the least democratic countries individual responsibility goes beyond mere submission. There is not a single country in our time where the government does not to some extent depend on public opinion. The personal response to present events becomes then the occasion for exercising the public authority God has instituted for our benefit, however restricted the means of action, however uncertain their effectiveness may be. Whatever the circumstances, our political responsibility will involve us in working toward the establishment of genuine freedom and justice, furnishing to the constituted authorities, to the government in particular, the instruments of regulation and coercion necessary to the maintenance of order.

If we restrict ourselves to this first theological perspective, we may well tend toward a conservative attitude to politics, more concerned with order than with progress, and risk slipping into the catholic error, the definition of a Christian political system. On the other hand, this theological insight gives us a better understanding of the serious danger of anarchy. I do not mean the political doctrine of that name, but the elementary disorder which always threatens in times of great political and social crisis. All those who have lived through one of these periods of spontaneous anarchy, in the course of military defeat, for instance, can testify to the disastrous consequences. Anarchy is probably the worst of political perversions, because it causes more suffering than any other, by shattering the order that God has instituted as a brake to our wickedness. It is in this light that we can understand the well-known comment by a member of the German Confessing Church: "When I see a Nazi policeman in the street, I thank God, for it is better to have some police, however bad, than none at all."

There can certainly be no question of absolutizing our duty of obedience to the authorities, if we hold to the biblical teaching. "We must obey God rather than man" (Acts 5:29). Nothing could ever free us from this obligation. It is our first concern and limits our political obedience. If the authorities, perverting their office, try to force us to disobey the Lord, our very concern for the maintenance of order compels us to refuse to obey them. This however never excuses us from our first task, to pray for these authorities and to ask God to lead them to a truer understanding of their powers and duties.

LOVE FOR THE NEIGHBOR

Politics is also for the Christian the opportunity to love his neighbor in practical ways, to help the suffering, to serve the "poor." The poor occupy an honored place in the Bible. Let us read again, for instance, the Magnificat, the old hymn which is prophetic of Jesus' ministry. "He who is mighty has done great things for me. . . . He has shown strength with his arm, he has scattered the proud . . . he has put down the mighty from their thrones, and exalted those of low degree; he has filled the hungry with good things, and the rich he has sent empty away" (Luke 1:49–53). Or the prophecy of the Last Judgment: "When the Son of man comes in his glory . . . he will sit on his glorious throne. Before him will be gathered all the nations, and he will separate them one from another as a shepherd separates the sheep from the goats, and he will place the sheep at his right hand, but the goats at the left. Then the King will say to those at his right hand, 'Come, O blessed of my Father, inherit the kingdom prepared for you . . .; for I was hungry and you gave me food, I was thirsty and you gave me drink, I was a stranger and you welcomed me, I was naked and you clothed me, I was sick and you visited me, I was in prison and you came to me.'" Then to the righteous who ask him when they have done all these things, he will answer, "As you did it to one of the least of these my brethren, you did it to me" (Matt. 25:31–40).

If we take seriously these two prophecies, can we remain indifferent to human suffering? We call ourselves Christians, disciples of him who healed the sick, fed those who hungered, loved those who suffered. Does this not imply that at all times we should bring help to the weak, the oppressed, to all the victims of this world? In face of the disasters that lay waste mankind today, individual charity seems inoperative. It can bandage only a few wounds, without ever attacking the disease itself. We live in a time when there seem to be no remedies for suffering whose origin is political, except political ones. Do we really want to "feed those who hunger, clothe those who are naked, welcome those who are alien"? Let us get to work then and help the victims of racial discrimination and economic exploitation, peoples subjected to foreign dominaton, prisoners, political refugees, deported people, those whom political propaganda deprives of their spiritual freedom, those willfully kept in ignorance that they may remain the docile instruments of a totalitarian state or of private interests anxious to secure cheap manpower. Think of the scandal of hunger from which two-thirds of humanity suffers, while a privileged minority cares about nothing but acquiring always greater abundance and more luxury. Nothing less than profound social and political reforms, nothing less than an economic revolution, nothing less than new international structures will change the lot of all these victims and deliver them from the anguish of the next day. In 1960, to love our fellow men means to engage in politics. To remain indifferent to politics, as do so many Christians even today, to repudiate this "social gospel" is to deny the Lord of the poor. Too numerous are those Christians who still imagine that they can do without economic and political transformations. They do not realize or refuse to reckon with the consequences of sin which are reflected in social organization, in political life, and in international relations. They rely hopefully, for the betterment of the human situation, on the general good will, on the fruits of personal conversion, and on the charity of the church. They do not admit that repentance and conversion should have direct consequences for our political conceptions. Their attitude, illustrated fairly well by Moral Rearmament, results in nothing more than providing at little cost a good conscience to those who, perhaps without realizing it, profit from the misery of others.

THE FREEDOM OF THE CHURCH

During recent years there has been a good deal of emphasis placed on another aspect of Christian ethics: the political authorities have

as their essential task to guarantee the freedom of the Church. I
have already quoted from Paul's first letter to Timothy. We must
now read an additional verse. If Paul requests prayer for the authorities
it is in order that "we may lead a quiet and peaceable life, godly and
respectful in every way," and also because "this is good, and it is
acceptable in the sight of God our Saviour, who desires all men to be
saved and to come to the knowledge of the truth" (I Tim. 2:2-4).
God wants man to live an honest, quiet, and peaceful life so that he
may hear the gospel and put it into practice. The crime of totalitarianism and of anarchy is that they annul all freedom of conscience. The
crime of social and economic injustice is to plunge man into
such misery that he no longer has ears to hear the gospel. Political
disorder effectively hinders the preaching of the Church. It deprives
the preaching of its meaning, because either the Church is prevented
from speaking, or men are prevented from listening. Since life has
no other purpose than to know Jesus Christ, to believe in him, and to
give him glory, evangelism—the proclamation of Jesus Christ—
gives history its true meaning. It is only for the sake of our witness
that God in his great patience still grants the world a little time.
We must thus be concerned before all else to see to it that the good
news of Jesus Christ is proclaimed and believed. Without this, nothing has any meaning.

Let us be precise. The issue here is simply that the Church must
have the freedom to preach the gospel, nothing else. The freedom
of the Church as such is not an absolute political criterion, but the
freedom to preach the gospel. Only the Church can know whether
it preaches this good news, and it is not the state's business to define
the limits of the Church's freedom. A church under persecution
must therefore undertake a serious self-examination before protest-
ing. Is it really being persecuted because of the gospel? The Church
has no right at all to demand an unconditional freedom. What is
the right, for example, on which we base our contention that we are
persecuted when the state deprives the Church of the right to hold
property? Does the freedom to witness necessarily imply the right
to organize Christian schools or hospitals? Prudence and discernment are certainly needed before we can make any judgment.

This freedom, furthermore, should not be viewed from an exclusively ecclesiastical angle, either. It is not enough that the Church
be granted the right to preach the gospel: men must be able to
listen to it and put it into practice. If political or economic condi-

tions prevent people from hearing and believing, there is persecution just as surely as when missionaries, evangelists, and pastors are thrown into prison. According to God's plan the authorities must be watchful that nothing interferes with either the preaching of the gospel or the faith of men.

This does not mean that the state should compel men to obey God. When the Roman Catholic Church opposes the legal recognition of divorce, it demands of the civil authorities more than they can grant. It would be inadmissable that the state should make of divorce an obligation, but we are in no way authorized to demand that the state prohibit it legally. All we may ask is that the state does not promulgate any law making disobedience to God compulsory, and that it never makes illegal anything which is in accordance with the will of God. We cannot ask the state to make illegal what God forbids us to do lest we dangerously confuse church and state, obedience in faith and fear of the police. The task of the state is nothing more, but also nothing less, than maintaining in the world not that order which should characterize the life of the Church, but that order which allows the Church to render witness to Jesus Christ by its words and by its life.

POLITICS AND THE KINGDOM OF GOD

We have already established the relations between a Christian political ethic and the hope for the Kingdom, that "new city" where there will be neither grief, nor tears, nor injustice, nor oppression, where all the disorders of the world, including the political disorders, will come to an end. This hope of the Kingdom is the motivation for and the content of our witness. I turn now to its political significance. I want to refer to the remarkable little book by Karl Barth, *The Christian Community and the Civil Community*, one of the best introductions to the political responsibility of the Christian. As on many other occasions, Barth makes use of analogy. The state "in relation to the Church," he writes, "is an independent reality: in relation to the Kingdom of God it is (like the Church itself) a human reality bearing the stamp of this fleeting world. It is therefore out of the question to identify State and Church on the one hand and State and Kingdom of God on the other. But from another perspective, since the State is based on a particular intention of divine grace and stands under the reign of Jesus Christ, it has no autonomy, and could not exist independently of the Church and the Kingdom of God. That is why one cannot speak of an *absolute difference* between State and Church on the one hand, and between State and Kingdom of God on the other. There remains only one possibility from the Christian point of view: the State and its justice are a parable, a correspondence, an analogy to the Kingdom of God. The State is capable of reflecting indirectly, as in a mirror, the truth and the reality of the Kingdom of God that the Church proclaims." But society and the state do not always present this reflection, this analogy of the Kingdom. "To be saved from degeneration and decay the civil community needs to be reminded of the requirements of this justice which it is supposed to represent. Again and again it needs to hear that story whose goal and content can help the State to become an analogy, a parable of the Kingdom of God, and permit it to accomplish the tasks of civil justice." It is the Church's privilege to know this story and therefore its task is to proclaim to the state the righteousness of the Kingdom which alone can give it by analogy an understanding of civil justice.

Barth illustrates this principle of analogy with many concrete examples. He does not try, as he repeatedly insists, to formulate general and permanent rules, which would be the very opposite of the concept of analogy. He simply wants to show the practical character of his thesis. Each one of us, moreover, without being a great theologian, can discover in the light of faith possible analogies between the Kingdom of God and our political task. We believe in a Kingdom of righteousness; then we cannot remain indifferent to all the injustices in the world. We must fight with all our strength to achieve greater social, economic, and international justice. This is how we witness to the Kingdom of God. We believe in a Kingdom where we shall forever be freed from the slavery of sin: then we cannot tolerate in the world any form of slavery, be it subjection of body or of spirit. We must fight that men may freely think, freely exercise their civil rights and help each other, and freely believe in and obey their Lord. In this way also we witness to the Kingdom. We believe in a Kingdom of peace where there will be neither hatred, nor fear, nor death anymore: then we cannot lightly accept class conflict, military or economic warfare. We must fight for peace. In this way also we proclaim the Kingdom of God. We could easily continue this list, deducing political consequences from each aspect of the Lordship of Christ. One could also proceed in the opposite way, examining the important political problems of our day in the light of the Kingdom of God in order to find out how God wills that we should proclaim his Kingdom through our political choices.

In brief, the Kingdom of God can serve both as guidance and as criterion for the Christian's political action. We are not, of course, building the Kingdom on earth, in history, by political means; for it is not of this world. It is rather that our thoughts, our words, and our actions must point in the direction of the Kingdom. Our task is to hold up signs of the hidden Kingdom whose ambassadors we are. These signs are at most very imperfect imitations, provisional and approximate, but nevertheless *significant* because their importance lies not in themselves, but in what they point to. Our task is, if you like, to become for our fellow men road signs to the Kingdom, accomplishing at one and the same time the work of politics and evangelization.

In this context provisional judgment can be made *hic et nunc* on various political systems. If we look at them as possible analogies with the Kingdom of Jesus Christ, a valid case can be made for many aspects of liberal democracy, not as a Christian solution, but as the best solution for the present moment, for instance in the Western world. For the same reason, in the underdeveloped countries, a case could perhaps be made against this same liberal democracy and for some more authoritarian form of government, simply because, through its inability to cope with the pressing material needs of these countries, liberal democracy ceases to be the kind of analogy with Christ's Kingdom which it appears to be in the West. But all such judgments can only be very relative and provisional; to build a system of political principles on this conception of analogies would be to deny its very basis, to substitute in fact an ontological relation for the analogical one. This, however, raises the whole question of the teaching ministry of the church in politics.

CHAPTER IV

The Political Ministry of the Church

The whole life of the Church must be devoted to witnessing to Jesus Christ and his Kingdom. However, it is logical for us to look first at the part played in evangelism by the teaching office of the church, its task of giving instruction to its members and to the world about God's truth and will. This teaching ministry is a form of evangelism; it is also responsible for defining the norms of evangelism, for correcting its content and methods, for reminding the church of the message it must proclaim.

INSTRUCTION WITHIN THE CHURCH

The teaching ministry is, of course, directed first to church members. The church hears the Word of God for the purpose of teaching it to its members, who must then put it into practice. Because the church has just rediscovered the Christian meaning of politics, it must instruct its members about this, especially since most of them are ignorant or confused about the place of politics in the plan of God. Not only are they unaware of the political demands of their faith. In most cases it does not occur to them that the Scriptures could teach them these things. In recent years great efforts have been made to prepare church members for political responsibility: Christian literature, study groups, training centers for the laity, youth movements, professional associations. But political instruction must be given more emphasis in the regular teaching activities of the church, in the parish, in the education of young people, in Sunday preaching, in catechism classes, and very especially in theological seminaries.

The teaching ministry of the Church cannot, of course, be limited to its own members. The Church is not responsible for itself alone; as the Church of Jesus Christ it is responsible for the whole of mankind. Jesus Christ came into the world for the world, not for the Church. His truth, the great truth of his love, of our creation, of his incarnation, of his second coming, the great and unbelievable truth of reconciliation and redemption, is for all men and must be proclaimed to all men. If the Church's teaching is not addressed to all men, if it is valid only for church members, it is no longer the teaching of Jesus Christ. This is true of teaching on personal morality, on pure theological doctrine, as well as on political ethics. This forces us to look at the second aspect of the ministry of the Word which I would term the Church's political ministry to those outside it. This has to do with the word which the Church addresses not so much to its own members as to people in the world and especially to those in offices of political authority.

ECCLESIASTICAL PRONOUNCEMENTS

I shall confine myself here to the public and official pronouncements made by properly constituted church bodies. Why this limitation? For practical reasons primarily, for such pronouncements as these at the present time are raising the most difficult problems. Whether the church speaks out or keeps silent, there will always be those who rise in protest. Some will accuse the church of torpor and indifference to worldly scandals and human suffering and ask for more pronouncements; others accuse it of overstepping its proper "spiritual" realm; and the church leaders do not know which way to turn. As a result, the work of synods and church assemblies takes on an incoherent character, the church often making solemn statements on insignificant subjects while remaining silent on crucial questions. And yet these practical difficulties are secondary. The unique importance of these official pronouncements of the church is theological, deriving from the authority which we grant or should grant them. True, the Word of God is never bound to any human institution, ecclesiastical or secular. If the organized church becomes unfaithful, either by its silence or by its all too human utterances, God can and often does speak through isolated Christians or even through the pagan world. And so it sometimes happens, when the churches are unfaithful, that God uses small groups that speak in a prophetic way to make his will known. This is particularly true in relation to political issues. Nevertheless it is the task of the church itself, in its institutional form, to state in solemn, official, and public pronouncements what God may have to say in the world about present political events. What is more, as Christians we owe a special respect to what our church thus declares. There is no question, certainly, of any doctrine of infallibility; no one on earth is infallible, not even the church. Every thought, every human word must be submitted to the biblical criterion; even ecclesiastical pronouncements may be heretical or simply mistaken. But as a rule we must *presume* them to be right. Humanly speaking, the church, through its official bodies, is more likely to speak in the name of the Lord than any individual Christian or any official group, gathered only provisionally, with a limited goal, and representing only a fraction of the church.

Let us recognize frankly that our confessional and denominational divisions create a serious problem. This fragmentation of the church should ultimately deprive it of its authority, but here, as elsewhere, it is impossible to draw logical conclusions from the division of the church, which is not only scandalous but a logical monstrosity. A divided church should be incapable of speaking with authority, of speaking the truth. But the truth of Jesus Christ is no dead system of concepts or maxims, it is a living person. This is why the church, in spite of its divisions, through the pure miracle of God, can still speak the divine truth.

Up to now I have been concerned more with what the church has omitted than with what it has committed in dealing with the Christian responsibility in political matters. In regard to official pronouncements, on the contrary, the church seems to be tempted to err more by excesses than by exaggerated caution. In the last few years our churches have perhaps abused these official declarations and have spoken up not only when they should have, but also when it was out of place to do so. The church should know how to be courageous, but also prudent. Prudence is a form of courage, and courage turns into temerity if it is exercised outside the domain of revelation on the shifting sands of human enthusiasms or prejudices. The church can speak; it receives this power from God. But should it speak? When should the church speak? When should it keep silent?

When political events threaten the essence of the gospel, when the state promulgates laws which undermine the very foundations of Christian faith and pervert the nature of the church, as was the case with Hitler's anti-Semitic regulations, the church has no other course but to protest officially and to reaffirm, in the face of political paganism, the fullness of the gospel, even going so far as to call its members to disobey the state. A church which fails to do so ceases to be the Church of Christ. This may be an extreme case; nevertheless the church must remain vigilant.

Today, for instance, it must ask itself seriously whether the threat of atomic warfare does not represent another such extreme case. The church should always examine political developments carefully to be sure that it does not betray the gospel by its silence. By remaining indifferent, or by upholding through silent agreement forms of manifest revolt against God, the church implicitly, and certainly unwillingly, speaks against Jesus Christ. On the other hand, such political events offer the church a wonderful opportunity to preach Jesus Christ, to evangelize. And past experience has shown that in this way the church both demonstrates its faithfulness and very effectively proclaims the gospel. But this can only happen if and when the church speaks in the name of Jesus Christ, because of him, and not because of its own human convictions or emotions, however noble and generous they may be.

It is not even enough to speak in accordance with the biblical revelation. It is *the Church* which must speak. I have referred to the privilege and duty of the official church institutions; but they must speak in the name of the Church, represent the consensus of those who believe in Jesus Christ. If such a consensus is lacking, if there is a disagreement among members of the church, this should always be taken as an alarm signal: Do we understand rightly the biblical teaching? Are we applying it correctly to the political situation?

On the other hand, in cases where it seems impossible to draw direct, logical, and unquestionable conclusions from the Scriptures, the existence of a real consensus among members of the church may authorize it to speak authoritatively about political events. When all Christians have come to a common mind about a political problem, it can be presumed that they are in the truth, for God does not leave the Church without his Spirit. But let us be cautious. This consensus must transcend denominational and national boundaries; especially in matters of international concern, churches should always consult together before speaking. The Church is one, and its consensus, to be valid, must be universal, even in the sense of historical continuity. The churches should not only consult together but look to the church fathers for instruction. Above all, we must beware of ecclesiastical nationalism. Too often our churches speak about current events without having consulted one another, even though the ecumenical movement provides the necessary channels of communication; unhappily, in some cases they even consider such consultation as intolerable interference in their own affairs, as if the problems of one member of the Church of Christ were not those of the whole community. "The body is one while having many members, and all members constitute the one body. . . . God has arranged the body . . . so that there should be no divisions in it, but that members be equally concerned one for another. When one member suffers all members suffer with it. You are the body of Christ" (I Cor. 12:*passim*).

INTERPRETING WHAT IS HAPPENING IN THE WORLD

Apart from these two instances—assault on the essence of the church by political authorities, and clear consensus among church members about a given issue—does the church have the right officially and publicly to express its opinion about political matters? To be even more precise, can the church legitimately go a step further and interpret contemporary events? God can indeed give it such wisdom and insight. As a rule, however, the church can only reaffirm the main lines of its theology of history, on the basis of which its members can proceed individually to a real analysis of events. I realize that on this point centers one of the main theological debates of our time. Most theologians agree that the Bible provides us with the elements of a theology of history. Their disagreement begins precisely with this question: Is a "Christian" interpretation of historical events possible and legitimate? When I say "Christian" I mean "normative for Christians." Everyone recognizes that the individual Christian has the right and even the duty personally to interpret history in the light of his own human wisdom.

I personally can conceive of no other normative knowledge of history than that for which the elements are given to us in the Bible. By this I mean the history of salvation fulfilled by Jesus Christ, from the Creation to his return in glory, of which the cross and the resurrection are the center. We know the meaning of history because we believe in salvation, because we live between the Ascension and Second Coming, in the time of the Church, which is the time of the Holy Spirit. We know that the ultimate significance of history is gathered up in the fact that it sets the stage for the drama of salvation. For the Church the meaning of history is the history of salvation, and no historical event can be understood outside of this perspective, and especially that of the coming Kingdom of God. But are we ourselves permitted to determine the place and role of particular events in the plan of God? Faith can discover in the perplexities of human history signs of divine providence. As a Christian historian or citizen I may discern a special and theological meaning in the political revolutions of our time. I may view them as God's judgment on his church's unfaithfulness or as one way he chooses for speaking to the world when the church keeps silent. Yet at the same time I know that another Christian may legitimately see in these same revolutions a sign of man's revolt against God, of Satan's unleashing. Is the church entitled to choose between these two interpretations or to attempt to reconcile them, recognizing a partial truth in each? It would seem to me that the church should rather admit the limits of its competence. The Church is not God. If it should claim to interpret history, it would soon be tempted to foretell the future course of events. It would thus do the very thing which it is forbidden to do, determining "the day and the hour" that no one may know except the Father (Matt. 24:36). We must "interpret the signs of the time" (Matt. 16:3). Yet these are nothing but signs, that is warnings addressed to us by God, but no foundation on which to construct a system. Their interpretation will always remain provisional, tentative, and therefore personal. It does not belong to the teaching ministry of the church, which on the contrary must be founded only on explicit biblical revelation.

A PASTORAL MINISTRY

Should the church as an institution then refrain from any reference to current political events? Certainly not. Even without venturing a theological interpretation of history, the church has an almost pastoral ministry to fulfill among the political authorities and the mass of citizens. We do know God's intentions for the world. The church has, therefore, the task of reminding not only the faithful, but all men and in particular those responsible for the government of nations, what their Lord intends for this world. The church cannot affirm without explanation that God wills this or that. Its political ministry is part of its task of witness; it must thus be carried on with the constant concern to proclaim the gospel in intelligible ways.

Let us take some examples. First, a situation of racial conflict. If the government carries out a policy of discrimination and segregation, the church has the duty to affirm both that in the Church there is neither Jew nor Greek, nor barbarian, nor man, nor woman, nor slave, nor free, nor white, nor black, and that the Church cannot tolerate within itself any form of discrimination. But it must also remind the state and society by speaking out and by example that God shows no partiality, is no "respecter of persons," that discrimination and segregation are therefore contrary to his will; in short that the earthly city can and should present an analogy of the Kingdom of God. But it is not within the church's competence to define the means, legislative, administrative, or educational, through which the necessary reforms should be achieved, and even less should it describe the exact content of such measures. Only under extreme circumstances does it have the right to put forward specific suggestions, and even then these suggestions must not be offered as a "Christian solution" to the problem, but only as a humble contribution to the common effort of society.

Let us consider another example. I mentioned above that the time may have come for the church unequivocally to condemn atomic weapons and refuse their use under any pretext whatsoever. But it does not seem to me to be within its province to define the exact terms of disarmament control. It must be ready to leave to the experts the search for practical and effective solutions and recognize that in most cases it is incompetent in technical matters of politics. Even before it officially condemns atomic warfare, the church should seek out the advice of scientific and military experts, withstanding the temptation to engage its authority at the prompting of a generous impulse, however noble it may be.

The last example I will take is painfully real for me: the Algerian conflict and the responsibility of my own church in it. Frankly, I am grateful that the French Reformed Church has thus far avoided proposing any solution to this tragic conflict. It is natural that in this domain the politicians should find a solution that is both just and workable. The French churches have, however, a great deal they can say without intervening in the technical field which is not their own. Could they not, for example, remind the French people that all men are equal before God, and hence apt to maintain that any solution in Algeria a fundamental inequality between Moslems and Europeans would be wrong and condemnable? Could they not reaffirm that God wishes all men to live together in peace an honest and quiet life, and hence that there can be no question of a political solution that would only perpetuate the conflict, even under the guise of "pacification" carried out by the army or police? Could they not point out that misery is as serious an evil as oppression, if not worse, and hence that any solution which would only guarantee civil rights without attacking the distressing economic and social problem of North Africa is inadmissible? Could they not speak up and tell the French people that, in the eyes of God, duties come before rights, and that instead of debating who is right or wrong in the Algerian conflict and whether there are acceptable negotiators on the other side, they should take immediate action to stop the massacre and alleviate the poverty? Are these recommendations too vague? And yet if they were taken seriously by the French government their concrete implications would immediately be obvious; even though they do not propose any clear-cut solution to the Algerian conflict, they rule out so many possible solutions that finally the choice is limited to a few variations of the same basic approach.

It is, as a matter of fact, in the very nature of the teaching ministry of the Church to be more negative than positive, to eliminate unacceptable solutions rather than formulate valid ones, precisely because it is the ministry of the Church and not a function of the state. One could draw a parallel here between the political and the doctrinal ministries of the Church. In matters of doctrine the Church in the last analysis only sets up the demarkation line between faith and heresy, determining the boundaries beyond which there is no belief in the God of Jesus Christ. It is impossible for theology ever to apprehend and describe the full reality of God. God is never the object, but always the subject of our knowledge. Yet theology has a rightful place, for by banishing all that does not belong to faith, it becomes the guide for faith. Similarly in the political realm the Church, without defining political solutions, can guide citizens and governments toward satisfactory or at least acceptable solutions simply by warning them of the errors to be avoided.

THE TEMPTATIONS OF THE CHURCH

In its political ministry the Church must take great care not to succumb to certain unavoidable temptations. First, the Church should guard against transforming itself into a pressure group, seeking to be heard because it represents a political force. Its only authority, the only reason it has for raising its voice to teach or to admonish, is that it speaks in the name of the Lord. If it were to speak in the name of the Lord *and* of a few million voters it would cease to be the Church of Jesus Christ and become simply a human organization, perhaps respectable and useful. But it would have lost its *raison d'être*, which is to render in the world witness to Jesus Christ.

The difficulty is real. The Church cannot be satisfied simply to speak, but must be concerned with the results of its pronouncements. When the Church teaches its members the meaning and importance of politics, it must call them to become personally involved in political action, to use every means at their disposal to get results. Therefore, even though the Church may not desire for itself any other authority than that of God's Word, it remains probable that the greater the political activity of its members, the greater will be its prestige with the state. There is, I believe, no theoretical solution to this dilemma. The Church must both speak in the name of Jesus Christ alone and yet also prepare its members for effective political service. It must continuously be careful in its official pronouncements never to use the political influence it in fact possesses because of the sheer number of Christians engaged in the struggle. But neither should the Church fall into a mistaken reticence. It is perfectly normal for the Church to remind its members of the means of action available to them, such as the right to vote, membership in a political party, letters to congressmen, groups for political education and information.

The Church owes it to itself to be especially prudent here because the world is always seeking its support. All political regimes, even those founded upon the separation of Church and state, even those which profess an explicit atheism, cherish the Church's approval. To quote just one example: In his presidential campaign of 1952 General Eisenhower, whose political and religious creed certainly includes the separation of Church and state, in speaking of the French situation deplored the fact that as a result of the dechristianization of France the Church could no longer serve as it should as the powerful and irreplaceable bulwark of the social and political order. Even Communist governments enjoy having the support of church dignitaries, in the non-Communist world or in their own countries.

If the world seeks the support of the Church, the Church with human frailty, likes very much to oblige. Quite apart from the ever-present temptation to defend the personal interests of its members, the Church loves to speak on political matters. Does it find it flattering to deal with important problems, to be listened to by more people than usual, to be associated with the powerful of this world? Or, to be more charitable, does it see there a real evangelistic opportunity?

In the midst of such temptations we must seek constantly to remain humble. Humble before men whose weaknesses and guilt we share; humble before our political leaders whose competence and honesty we often doubt unjustly, not realizing the fearful complexity of their task nor the obstacles they have to overcome; humble above all before God whose unprofitable servants we are. The greatest danger that threatens the Church in carrying out its political ministry is the temptation of taking itself too seriously, of giving too great an importance to this ministry and the fruits it may bear. The future of the world is not in the hands of men, not even in those of the Church, for God himself is taking care of it. But above all the ultimate meaning of this ministry lies in witness. This ministry is significant not because it can help to avoid some historical catastrophy, but because through it the gospel may be preached. This missionary intention is, moreover, the only safeguard, the only discipline which permits us to withstand the temptation of pride. If we understand the political ministry of the Church as an important part, but still only as a part of the total task of evangelization, we may more easily avoid the dangers of prestige, power, and conformity. For the evangelistic nature of the Church's prophetic task recalls us to the fundamental concern not for ourselves or the Church or for politics, but for the Kingdom of God and his righteousness.

THE CHURCH'S TASK OF STUDY

Perhaps I have given too cautious a description of the Church's political ministry, traced too severely its limit, and thus condemned it to confine itself to generalities very foreign to our daily preoccupations. I am aware of this and I understand very well those who, day by day faced with the inextricable complications of political problems, call on the Church for help. I wish only to say that so far I have only dealt with the public and official ministry of the Church as it is carried out by the voice of its properly constituted bodies. There is room for complementary political activities in education, research, counseling, for the benefit both of church members and society as a whole. In a sense this brief essay is an illustration of the possibility of Christian reflection about politics that is neither part of the official teaching ministry of the Church nor a purely personal judgment on political life. While the theological rediscovery of politics was under way, the churches in many places undertook to organize groups to carry on political studies, agencies for social service, and channels for international contact. These groups are too numerous to be counted. Some of these groups sprang up spontaneously, initiated by a few Christians particularly concerned about their faithfulness in the political sphere. Others were officially set up by church authorities. Some groups function within one church; others work in a much freer way, often interconfessionally and in some instances even wholly under lay leadership. Some are exclusively Christian, others are open to anyone. All are involved in political thinking, and sometimes political action, being generally careful not to speak in the name of the Church, not to commit its authority, and not to evolve into Christian political parties. They are simply trying to carry the ethical teaching of the Church further than can be done officially. They group Christians driven by the same preoccupation with politics and desirous to study together the most important or complex political questions. Their reports or resolutions are obviously not normative for Christian political thinking; their only claim to authority lies in the serious work that has gone into the studies. Nevertheless, their lack of political bias and their explicit base in biblical ethics make them very valuable guides, and we might wish the churches would do more along this line.

Should not the churches themselves, however, set up working commissions—functioning on an intermediary level between the official teaching ministry of the Church and personal involvement in politics —that would deal with the thousands of questions about which Christians are calling for help both of theologians and political experts? The Commission of the Churches on International Affairs, under the joint auspices of the World Council of Churches and the International Missionary Council, is a good example. The CCIA has been criticized for not having always made sufficiently clear whether it spoke with the authority of the Church or simply with the wisdom of competent theologians and political experts. Sometimes its reports have been too exclusively political and have lacked an explicit theological foundation. Nevertheless, all churches might profitably follow this example, and many have already done so by establishing on the national level specialized commissions to deal with international problems and other aspects of political, economic, and social life.

It is impossible to overestimate the evangelistic significance of these efforts. We cannot compile statistics on conversions; it is not in our power to establish a scale of evangelistic efficiency for the various forms of the Church's ministry. However, there is abundant evidence that many have heard and understood something of the Christian message through the political studies and publications of all sorts of Christian groups. On the other hand, it is impossible to overestimate the dangers of this ministry. How many have been turned away from the Church, even from Jesus Christ, because the churches or their members spoke irresponsibly about politics, or kept silent when they should have spoken.

CHAPTER V

Political Action as the Language of Evangelism

So far I have hardly spoken at all about direct personal engagement in politics. Yet most Christians find this to be the best opportunity for witness in the political field.

In a previous chapter I discussed the two temptations we must confront, the two heresies, contradictory yet complementary, of pietism and catholicism. I pointed out that while the former withdraws from the world and politics, the latter views politics as a means for Christianization or ecclesiastical conquest. On a more personal level pietism is apt to lean naturally toward an attitude of neutrality in politics, whereas catholicism willingly chooses the road of the Christian political party whose task is seen as the elaboration and more especially the implementation of a Christian program. I shall not again go into the intrinsic theological error of these attitudes, but instead I shall now try to show their practical consequences.

I. THE ILLUSION OF NEUTRALISM

I already pointed out the illusory character of neutrality. I do not refer here to the specific choice, to the unique political program that the neutrality of a country can represent internationally. Swiss neutrality has proved its worth, and it would be utterly unjust to see it as political indifference, since neutrality in this sense constitutes a clear political decision. Similarly those nations like India who seek today to preserve their independence, between the Atlantic powers and the Communist powers, by way of a "positive neutrality," are simply choosing the political strategy of the "third force." The term neutrality does not apply to their attitude toward politics in general, but only to specific political powers.

In speaking of the illusory character of neutrality, I refer only to the pietist temptation. For in pietism are the germs of a much more profound neutrality, of a real and fundamental indifference to politics, of the refusal to distinguish between various political positions and therefore to be committed to any of them. But what an utter illusion this is! Even the most elementary knowledge of history discloses the fallacy of such withdrawal. The hard fact is that in refusing to act politically, we are in fact engaging in a very definite political action. Political neutrality amounts to political conservatism. By remaining detached from current developments, we implicitly give our support to the *status quo*, to the powerful of this world. In France, under the Nazi occupation, political neutrality meant giving Hitler or the Vichy Government the very help they were seeking. These rulers, incidentally, were clever enough to concentrate on gaining the neutrality of the French people rather than trying to win them to the Fascist cause. Political neutrality in a Communist country means endorsing the Communist regime, not with the lips but with the heart. Political neutrality in a liberal democracy means rubber-stamping all social injustices.

I certainly do not suggest any condemnation of pacifism or passive resistance. The pacifist and the follower of Gandhi are not politically neutral. They make a clear political choice. They reject violence. They also fight, but with means that are different from those ordinarily used in politics. True neutrality, the refusal to take politics seriously and to accept some responsibility in it, results actually in making us conspirators with evil. Nothing reveals more clearly the illusory character of neutrality; for exactly those who see in politics one of the most cynical manifestations of sin and refuse to be mixed up with it, actually end up much against their will supporting the most scandalous forms of it.

What is then the evangelistic significance of such a refusal? When the church refuses to be interested in politics, when Christians turn away from political action, do they not in practice deny the very

message they proclaim? Or does this mean that it is not possible to
act politically as Christians?

In recent years many Christians who in no way share the pietistic
conception of the world have revived the question of neutrality in a
variety of ways. In a world in progressive deterioration, where political action seems destined to fail, where totalitarianism infiltrates
into seemingly democratic regimes, is there any possibility of choice
left to the Christian, since all proposed solutions seem equally unacceptable? The diabolical character of totalitarian regimes finds here
its finest expression. In order to resist them, democracy itself slides
slowly toward totalitarianism or at least uses totalitarian methods
as the only effective weapons for its own defense. It has been said
of Hitler that his most evil work was that he corrupted even his
enemies. Under these conditions can the Christian participate in the
battle? If truly there is no choice except between equally disastrous
alternatives, is not neutrality mandatory? My first reply is one of
caution. We must not too quickly throw in the sponge. We must not
too quickly pass final condemnation on the whole gamut of politically viable solutions. There is room first of all for a detailed, serious
study to be undertaken without preconceived ideas. Furthermore,
even though all these solutions should really be unacceptable, our
first obligation would be to search for new and untried ones. We
cannot easily decide that the plight of the world is desperate, for
despair is as unchristian as is humanist hope.

Imagination is needed, but of course we must be realistic as we try
to formulate new solutions. Too well known are the many political
committees of the past whose good intentions were the common root
for both their merits and their ineffectiveness. Political idealism is
not only useless but dangerous and irresponsible, a denial of the
gospel we preach. For instance, to work for a world government is
to evade our political responsibility: a world government is today
impracticable; but other forms of international relations are more
immediately feasible. Even if world government were an ideal solution, even if it might one day be realized, it is not the way in which
today we can love our neighbor and help him in his suffering. Per-
fectionism is one of the worst political temptations.

It remains true that a political conjunction may force on the
Christian equally inadmissible choices. Even if the possibility presents
itself only rarely, in times of acute crisis, it is a real one. Must we
then resort to political indifference and neutrality? Certainly not.

When the Church finds itself in the midst of an unleashing of violence, injustice, and oppression, when the entire political life takes on a demonic character, as described in Revelation, then the Church is reduced to the only form of political action still left to it: to pronounce in the name of the Lord an unequivocal condemnation of all parties, governments, ideologies, because all represent man's revolt against his Creator. Such a condemnation could be costly to the Church, could send it back to the catacombs. It nevertheless remains a high form of political responsibility and the very opposite of neutralism.

II. CHRISTIAN POLITICAL PARTIES

I hold that political neutrality is an illusion. The catholic solution of the Christian party, although at least as evil as neutrality, if not more so, has nothing illusory about it, as the political history of the twentieth century clearly demonstrates. The proliferation of confessional or interconfessional parties, particularly in Europe, constitutes one of the essential factors in the postwar period. I should like to call to mind at least some of the consequences of their emergence. France at the time of Liberation placed high hopes in the MRP,[1] seeing in it the symbol and the means for an evolution of French catholicism toward less reactionary social and political expressions. These hopes have been disappointed, and we should not hide from ourselves the influence of the catholic parties on the political history of the last ten years. To cite the MRP again, its responsibility in the conflict in Indochina and in the 1947 repression in Madagascar is sadly evident. Christian democratic forces—or rather catholic democratic forces—played a decisive role in all the efforts for the integration of Europe. They have also contributed to the outbreak and perpetuation of the cold war between the Western world, which with a certain hypocrisy we call the "free world," and the Communist bloc. We must therefore pay serious attention to this comparatively recent phenomenon of the Christian political party, especially since it appears in Protestant just as well as in Catholic circles. The CDU, the Christian Democratic Union in West Germany, enjoys the support of the Protestant as well as the

[1] The Popular Republican Movement, formed as a new, moderately liberal political party at that time.

Catholic bourgeoisie. In Holland the conservative Protestant parties were started back in the last century.

It would be unjust to deny that these Christian political parties, at least in their origin, were the expression of a sincere and commendable desire for renewal. Their multiplication is partly the result of a well thought-out strategy of the Vatican, linked perhaps with Rome's other major political move, the anti-Communist crusade. But their success is just as much bound up with the decadence of the traditional parties. If so many Christians in Europe, both Catholic and Protestant, welcomed the Christian political parties with such enthusiasm, it was because the old parties, conservative, radical, socialist, or Communist, had brought them nothing but disappointment, had disgusted them with their mediocrity, their impotence, and their corruption. It was in order to do something new, to break out of the vicious circle of old partisan traditions that generous-hearted Christians so often rallied to form a Christian party.

Their one error consisted precisely in the fact that they based this effort of renewal on a grouping of Christian forces around a program presumed to be Christian. In other cases, aware of these dangers, young Christians have tried the experiment of associating themselves in new political formations with secular groups that were prepared to accept their program but did not share their faith. I mention as an example of this the organization of the labor party in Holland in which not only young Christians give leadership but also humanists, socialists, and all sorts of others. In France the MRP in its very beginnings represented exactly this sort of effort. Unfortunately, in accepting the support of the ecclesiastical hierarchy and the defense of purely confessional causes such as state aid to parochial schools, it degraded itself into a confessional party. Today, although its title does not mention this characteristic, the MRP represents in actual fact a Catholic political party.

THEOLOGICAL AMBIGUITY

When I speak of the theological ambiguity inherent in Christian political parties, I can speak only as a Protestant. My objection would not make sense to a Catholic. I may sum it up in one question already raised in a previous chapter. Does the nature of biblical revelation permit us to define the elements of a Christian civilization, of a

Christian political order or program? If we maintain that the Christian ethic, fruit of faith, varies according to times and circumstances; if we exclude the possibility of any casuistic code; if we understand political action as a witness to the Kingdom of God; if the relationship between this Kingdom and the earthly city is one only of analogy, then we must admit in principle that there is the possibility for Christians to obey their Lord in different ways. This rules out the concept of a Christian value system and with it the concept of a Christian political program. Since our obedience will never be more than a poor imitation, an imperfect sketch of the Kingdom of God and its holiness, there is room in the world for many different sketches. Like artists who paint their common model each from a different angle without any one person being able to bring its full beauty and life to the canvas, so the Christians, united both in their common expectation of the Kingdom and in their vocation to be its witnesses, can never manifest more than certain of its aspects as they go forward in their everyday obedience, and especially in their political service. Nor can they, in their human frailty, give more than an unfaithful imitation of the Kingdom.

Conversely, the concept of Christian political parties presupposes at least the possibility of some sort of ontological continuity between the Kingdom of God and the earthly city, and a possibility for the church logically to deduce the elements of a political program and of a civilization which it can tag with a label, "Christian." Such a theological view repudiates or at least hides under a bushel the eschatological hope as put forth in the Bible. Christian eschatology leaves no room whatever for the notion of either a Christian civilization or a Christian political party.

POLITICAL PARTIES AND THE UNITY OF THE CHURCH

Is it possible to fall back on a second position of defense and think of a party bearing the Christian name because it is in fact made up of Christians whose political choices, without directly and logically proceeding from their theological convictions, are nevertheless illumined by the same faith? My objection to this second definition of a Christian party would be that it abuses the name "Christian." Once and for all, we would be well advised to be more reserved, more discreet in the use of the term "Christian." Actually we should employ it only in two cases: as a description of the community of the faithful, and to qualify the faith, the thought, and the life of the church. We have no right whatever to put the Christian label on our individual activities, however generous these may be. Otherwise we might as well speak of a "Christian" grocery store if the owner or the manager happens to be a church member, or of "Christian" literature as referring to all novels whose authors are Protestant or Catholic, regardless of how secular the subject or the intentions may be.

Yet I would not want to give the impression that I have nothing but a quarrel over words with the Christian political parties. The betrayal of trust which the term "Christian party" represents is due more to the fact that it endangers the unity of the Church. It is bound to suggest the exclusion from the Christian community of all those who share the faith of the Church but nevertheless do not adopt the program of the Christian political party. Every Christian party calls for or implies the excommunication of its adversaries, those suspect of political heresy. I come back here to my first objection: if it is impossible logically to deduce from biblical revelation one political program to the exclusion of all others, then no party has the right to claim for itself a monopoly on Christianity and to imply that all who disagree with it politically are potential heretics.

I do not believe I exaggerate. When, for example, the Catholic parties in Europe, with the blessing of the church, take on the defense of economic liberalism against socialism, I cannot help seeing in this the insinuation that a socialist economy is wholly wrong from a Christian point of view and that the socialists are at best second-class Christians. When the Christian parties support the efforts toward European integration, they perhaps hurt the cause more than they help it by transforming a political discussion into a confessional controversy, implying that it is a betrayal of the Christian faith to hold different views of the future of Europe. In an altogether different political perspective, the Christian Democratic Union in Eastern Germany, also claiming to be a Christian party, inevitably tears apart the church by associating itself with the defense of the regime in the people's democracy.

To sum up, it seems to me that the concept of the Christian political party inevitably leads to that of a crusade. When the church tolerates being represented even indirectly by a politically oriented group, it is very near to putting itself at the service of particular political ambitions and to utilizing political means to further its own ends. A Christian political party tends inevitably to identify the mission of the Church in the world with the political struggle, with the service of a particular regime, with the fight against an enemy where it becomes unclear whether society or the church is threatened.

Finally, a word about the repercussions of Christian parties on evangelism. Far from helping the church to preach the gospel, they have been in recent years one of its heaviest liabilities. The cry of Spanish workers during the civil war, "Down with the Church—Christ with us," is well known. How often today ought we to hear a similar cry, "Down with this Christian party—Christ with us!" But, alas, we hear it less and less frequently. When people do shout it out, they prove that they have really heard the gospel. Today the harvest reaped by the Christian parties may be greater power for the church but greater indifference to Jesus Christ.

III. FORMS OF RESPONSIBLE PARTICIPATION IN POLITICAL LIFE

SOCIAL SERVICE

I have assumed that political action is not only an obligation but also an effective possibility for the Christian. What form should it take? By and large we can see it as a form of *diakonia,* of the service ministry of the Church to men, one of the ways in which Christians love their neighbors. This view sets some of the limits of political action. It can never be considered as *the* way, the only way, in which we fulfill our diaconal responsibility. Social service rather is the most natural response to the second commandment, starting, of course, within the Church but never limited to it; those who share our faith are our neighbors par excellence, but in every man we can and ought to see our neighbor, the image of Jesus Christ.

What form will *diakonia* take? It is worth looking at its place in the early church of Jerusalem, at the "primitive communism" which has so little in common with modern socialism but even less' with church life in our day. The Church of Jerusalem stands as a judgment on our failures, as an incentive for us to seek ways in which we can render real mutual service in the church. What a revolutionary example our churches would give today were they to practice "Christian communism"! What a ferment of renewal they would bring to society! What effective political instruments they would be! Above all, what hope there would be that our churches might regain their powerful evangelistic zeal and the contact with men which they so sadly lack today!

However, we must not be literalists. We are not called to imitate the primitive church, but Jesus Christ, and here again imagination is needed. We are frequently tempted, particularly in social service, to carry on along traditional lines, without examining whether forms which had meaning in another age are still valid. Is it not paradoxical that Christians often complain that the welfare state has taken over the diaconal work of the church? Should we criticize the state because it is now doing a better job of social service? Should we long to return to a society in which the poor could count on no help but personal or ecclesiastical charity? And how can we dare to say that even in the most highly developed welfare state we have no diaconal responsibility? Is it not the task of the church, especially in the welfare state, to serve the many who are just outside the normal categories, the outcasts of their age? And even when material needs have been satisfied, how much misery remains which no one else can alleviate? Such attacks on the welfare state are rather a political reaction or else they reflect the subconscious frustration of a church which has been deprived of certain functions which gave it social prestige—as if the Church needed a human justification for its existence! Our churches have certainly done much, even judged by human standards, through their hospitals, schools, old people's homes; but, in some countries, such services are no longer needed. We should rejoice and find new ways to serve within the structure of the state or of secular society.

There is no reason why Christian social service should be placed under church auspices. On the contrary, there is a tremendous value for evangelism in co-operation with non-Christians. For years the World's Student Christian Federation has shared with other religious and secular groups in a common enterprise of student relief; in order to do this it gave up its separate Christian relief program. Experience has shown not only the practical advantages of this unified approach but also its real missionary power. Those with whom we co-operated were better helped to understand that Jesus Christ alone was our motivation than would have been the case had we organized our own relief department. The danger of social service under Christian auspices has always been the making of "rice Christians"; it is hard for the church to make clear that it gives freely, as it has freely received from God, and that material aid is not a concealed way of buying conversions and building up church membership. However, it is possible to avoid this danger. The wonderful experience of the CIMADE (Comité Inter-Mouvement Auprès Des Evacués) in France, during and since the Second World War, shows that real evangelism can be effectively combined with Christian social service. But when CIMADE teams carried on their work of evangelism and material assistance in concentration camps, in prisons, among deportees, and in destroyed cities, they always had to make clear that participation in their religious activities was in no way a condition for receiving material help. Since the war the same principles have informed CIMADE's social work and evangelization among refugees from the East, in the French prisons, among students, and among North Africans, in short wherever modern society heaps material misery upon spiritual bewilderment. The CIMADE experiment is further worth our serious attention as it has always been carried on at the frontiers where in new and unforseen ways the church meets the modern world, in particular the political world.

Social service is essential to the church. Without it the political action of its members, all its teaching about politics will be in vain, and look like so much hypocritical self-righteous verbiage, or a screen for merely human concerns; without it the witness of the church to the love of Christ for all men will be effectively denied by the indifference of Christians to human suffering.

On the other hand, all acts of kindness, of assistance, of charity to those who suffer, will create those mysterious bonds which the Bible calls "neighborliness" and through which men see in one another the living image of the suffering Lord and the living proclamation of the gospel.

OTHER FORMS OF RESPONSIBLE INVOLVEMENT

How many Christians consider the civil service, public administration, justice, education, and all such aspects of public life, which tend to multiply in the modern state, as ministries instituted by God? In principle, when we study Romans 13, we speak of the "authorities" as instituted by God, but we seldom relate this to the many forms of public service in our time. Students rarely choose to prepare themselves for one of these professions because they are divinely instituted, but rather because of their own personal tastes or the advantages of such a career. The same can be said of other aspects of political, social, and economic life: labor unions, managerial associations, the press and radio, television, the cinema, and even those great commercial and industrial companies whose very size makes them a factor in politics. Christians should be taught that work in such fields is part of the political responsibility God has placed on his Church and therefore part of its missionary obligation.

PERSONAL INVOLVEMENT IN POLITICAL PARTIES

Let us now turn to political action, properly speaking. The majority of Christians in all parts of the world simply ignore it. Leaving aside for the moment those Christians who choose abstention and those who support Christian political parties, the great majority of the remainder either shrink from direct personal involvement in politics or participate fully in it, but as if their Christian faith were something quite irrelevant. In neither case does the politics-evangelism relationship exist.

The biblical foundations of Christian political ethics, while closing the door to Christian political parties, throw it wide open for active participation in non-Christian political parties. Christians are impelled to undertake such service as long as program and methods, of course, do not erect an impossible obstacle for our witness.

I would urge them to participate in already existing secular political groups, or to create new ones. No doubt, in our modern societies individual political action is vain; only the group has power. But how few Christians are willing to make the leap and to join a party! Several interesting and rather successful attempts to renew European political life were made after 1945 and Christians often took part in them: I am thinking, for instance, of the Dutch labor party and of the early days of the French MRP; in both cases the initiative came from Christians, but Christians who were aware of the dangers of political confessionalism and who systematically sought co-operation with non-Christians. Unfortunately, the MRP soon deteriorated into a crypto-confessional group. This illustrates the dangers of such a venture, but also that it is not impossible to create a new party. Therefore, when Christians are unable to find a satisfactory program and party, they should not exclude the possibility of creating and building up something new. But in most cases they will join existing parties within which they will try to serve and witness. How should we do this? I cannot give any concrete advice to those who

have to choose a party in which to take up their political responsibilities, for here we clearly enter the domain of personal decision,
of hazardous judgment, of convergent forces and of the remedies
they require. I shall therefore only point up certain more general
considerations which should guide us regardless of our political
affiliation.

IV. THE ETHICAL PROBLEMS OF POLITICAL ACTION

Our political action must reflect our Christian faith. If our service
is to witness to Jesus Christ, he must be present in our every action
and it is precisely here that the difficulties begin.

IMPOSSIBLE LOYALTIES

How far, for instance, can our faithfulness, our loyalty go toward
the political party to which we belong? Let us be clear on this. Never
for a Christian can the purpose of his political activity be limited to
or summed up in the success of a system, an ideology, or a party.
Never should the tactical interests of our party make us forget our
responsibility toward all men, toward the community which we try
to serve by political means. The party, its organization, structure,
and program, can never be anything more than the instruments we
use to serve a cause that goes way beyond them. We must always
be ready to sacrifice the instrument to the cause if the necessity
arises. In a sense, therefore, the Christian cannot join a political
party except with certain reservations. The party, like any human
organization, inevitably tends more and more to find in itself its own
justification, and the Christian will always have to remain somewhat apart from his fellows in the struggle. He can give only a
provisional adherence to the party program, only a limited, always
re-examined, loyalty to the party machinery.

We are faced with a similar problem in the whole conception of
patriotism. We ought to love our country. If we don't love the homeland that we see, how can we love the heavenly homeland in which
we believe? Or, to reverse it, how can we witness to the Kingdom of
God without expressing our affection for our native land, for the
people that have nourished us? And yet the Christian will never feel
quite at ease when people talk to him about patriotism. Even without carrying this so far as an aggressive and exclusive nationalism,

we cannot avoid the ambiguity inherent in our situation as Christians, our dual citizenship, in heaven and on earth. Sincere as our love for our country may be, we cannot give it an unlimited devotion. The possibility is always there that national patriotism could become contradictory to Christian faithfulness, for example, if it imperils the unity of the Church or results in oppression or injustices toward other peoples. Even more than patriotism I fear the idea of national loyalism which has become so current lately, perhaps under the influence of the Anglo-Saxon world where the term itself originated. (In the last century, the term "loyal" was almost exclusively used to describe personal relationships. Even when used in other ways it kept its etymological meaning of "respectful of the law.") Loyalism implies an unconditional devotion to which the Christian can never pledge himself. Whether in relation to the nation, regime, or political party, our allegiance or loyalty remains always subject to the unequivocal teaching of the gospel. "It is better to obey God than man" (Acts 5:29). As Christians we are forbidden to love, to commit ourselves, to bind ourselves to any human community as other people do. "If anyone comes to me and does not hate his own father and mother and wife and children and brothers and sisters, yes, even his own life, he cannot be my disciple" (Luke 14:26). If Jesus speaks with such severity of our least selfish human affections, should we not be just that much more careful in regard to national or political loyalism? The concept of loyalism includes a faithfulness which God alone can require of us. Let us note, in this regard, that we have no justification either for accepting as legitimate any confessional loyalism, which is so often the issue in ecumenical controversies today. Whatever the value to which we grant our loyalism, it will inevitably take on a religious and sacred character, and lead us to a total commitment which we owe to our Lord alone. It is significant moreover that the term "loyalism," referring to the political sphere, dates from the twentieth century which invented totalitarianism.

I am certainly not pleading for disloyalty. Much as loyalism and loyalty may border on each other, they are nevertheless radically different. Loyalty is really a form of honesty. In political matters, in relation to the party or the nation, our loyalty will consist precisely in not hiding that as Christians we reject loyalism; that our participation in party activities, our devotion to our country will always be limited by our loyalism or absolute loyalty to God. In making clear the nature of this limitation on our political involvement we can demonstrate how total is our dependence upon God, and proclaim that Jesus Christ is Lord.

THE CHRISTIAN AS A REVOLUTIONARY

Is this to say that we should view involvement in a political party as a questionable or perhaps even forbidden form of action? I do not think so. On the contrary, I regret that so many Christians refuse to become thus involved. I have described political action as service and witness. These two obligations are inseparable, but in daily political life they are in sharp contradiction. We must *witness* to Jesus Christ: therefore we must preserve the purity of the gospel and repudiate all compromise with human sin or wisdom. We must love our neighbor and *serve* him: therefore we must aim at political effectiveness. If we are unfaithful, our service loses its missionary significance, it no longer proclaims the Kingdom of God; if our service is ineffective and fails to improve human conditions politically and socially, we contradict our witness by tolerating human suffering and being incapable of alleviating it.

Let us suppose, for example, that we should come out in favor of the Atlantic Charter and its program of liberation, that we should give the sanction of our faith to these human freedoms. If we should not find effective ways of making this ideal into something more than words, we would be nothing more than hypocrites and liars; we would deny Jesus Christ. Our political action ought to change something in this world. That is one of the first criteria. The transformation will of course never be sufficient or complete; there will always be injustice and violence; there will always be the poor. Always, therefore, the Christian has to take up the struggle anew both through politics and through charity. Never can he be satisfied with the results obtained, but must ever and again renew his critical appraisal. Always he will be a "revolutionary," not in the usual sense with all it implies of secular idealism, but in the true sense of the word; he knows he must transform the world, fight against what is wrong and try to do better.

This revolutionary attitude of the Christian brings us back to the missionary significance of our political involvement. If we cannot possibly be satisfied with the results achieved, even though these be the fruits of our own efforts, it is because the criterion of our action is the content of our hope. When we act we seek to witness to the

Kingdom of God, the heavenly city which partakes of the holiness of its King and thereby condemns the highest human achievements, including those inspired by the coming Kingdom. With the vision of the Kingdom as our guide, we could not do otherwise—to use a political term—than to remain in the opposition, not necessarily in opposition to the government, but in opposition to the established order. Whether we employ the progressive and peaceful means of reforms or whether we resort to revolutionary violence, we will always be counted among the protesters, the discontent. Our task lies always ahead of us; it is never finished. I am perhaps describing a sort of Christian messianism somewhat similar to that which the people of Israel have so often manifested politically. Are we not also the people of the Messiah? We know that he has already come, yet we are awaiting his return, and this expectation commands our political action, gives it its uniqueness. Were we to lose this messianic expectancy, we would cease to render witness to God's Kingdom through our involvement in the world.

EFFECTIVENESS AND PURITY

To love our neighbor is to tell him of the Kingdom which is offered to him, but it is also to give him, starting today, bread, clothing, a home, an education, peace, and freedom. We have to act effectively. This, by the way, is why we must act politically, since in our day, as we have seen, individual action not only is impotent to eliminate the causes of human suffering, but can do little even to alleviate it.

We cannot avoid running head on into this clash of conscience in our political action: effectiveness and purity are contradictory demands. I shall refer once more to the experience of the underground Resistance during Hitler's occupation of France. In choosing to work out our obedience in the Resistance, we had to live daily with the dilemma of effectiveness and purity or, if you prefer, of ends and means. In resisting we hoped to be faithful witnesses of Jesus Christ; but by so doing we undertook to lie, to steal, to kill, to create disorder, all in contradiction to the demands of God's holiness, and hence perhaps invalidating the witness we were so desirous to render. But we did not have the choice between means that were worthy of their end and others that were not; we had to choose between resistance and collaboration. If we had refused the methods of the underground fight, we would have become entirely ineffective and perhaps even endangered those alongside whom we fought; if we had refused to take any part in the struggle, we would have surrendered to Nazi totalitarianism and acquiesced in all its atrocities. We were compelled to make an impossible choice. Perhaps after all we gave a bad witness. We were not able however to discover any clear-cut solution which would have allowed us to fulfill, at the same time, the double demand upon us for a faithfulness that is pure and uncompromised, and for effective service. Any Christian politician, moreover, goes through the same experience day after day, though in a less acute form. Political action is not possible without compromise. To act effectively in the midst of a sinful world, we have to make up our minds to use methods which we would never accept in the area of personal ethics. Violence, in particular, always characterizes all political action in one way or another.

WAR

This leads me to raise a problem that has always tormented the Christian conscience: war. I would like to discuss it in personal terms and tell you the answer, or rather the answers, which I have given to the fundamental question that is involved here: Can the Christian ever consider war as an acceptable solution to political problems? It does not do any good to take refuge behind the too easy alibi of a distinction between "defensive war" and "offensive war." Almost all Christians are certainly agreed today in condemning any clear aggression. The truly moral problem concerning war begins precisely when we can find justifiable reasons for war. Moreover, the history of this century has highlighted all too well the difficulty in a particular case of applying the theoretical distinction between aggression and legitimate defense. The political complexity of our day always leaves room for the adversaries in question to discuss endlessly who is responsible for what, and most often each one of them considers himself to be the victim of aggression.

In 1939 I chose war, without joy or good conscience, but unhesitatingly. I was convinced not only that there was no other viable political solution, but also that I had no other choice as a Christian. From 1940 to 1944 I chose the underground Resistance, knowing, however, that I was assuming before God the terrible responsibility for disorder, violence, and hatred. On the contrary, today, in 1960, faced with the threat of atomic war, I refuse to accept it as an eventuality; I fight against all fatalism about war and hold personally that peace is the only spiritual and political possibility, whatever the price we may have to pay for it. Why two such apparently contradictory attitudes only a few years apart? For reasons of political judgment. In 1939 or 1940 I could really expect positive results from the war or from the Resistance. Humanly speaking, they offered some chance for success in the establishment of a new political and social order, imperfect, but certainly better or in any case much less evil than the Hitlerian horror. Today, on the contrary, with the destructive weapons that modern armies have at their disposal, I cannot see how a world war could produce anything but universal destruction, complete chaos, terrible moral corruption, in short a situation much worse than the worst injustices which would have provoked war. If a war is to be morally bearable, it is necessary to see in it not the good, of course, but at least a lesser evil, a means of replacing an evil order or entrenched disorder by a better or more stable one. In its cruel and dangerous way war must be able to help re-establish or preserve in the world an order that conforms to the will of God. It is precisely at this point that the atomic discoveries seem to me to have changed the data of the problem. I do not suggest that it is less horrible to kill people with "classical arms" than to kill with atomic weapons.

In contrast to "classical wars," and perhaps still today in contrast to localized conflicts, atomic war wipes out all reasonable hopes for a livable postwar world. It seems probable that victors and victims—and we might well ask whether there will still be any victors—will be faced with such widespread material destruction, such political chaos, a moral and cultural crisis of such dimensions, that it will not be possible to speak of order, let alone raising the question as to whether it accords to the will of God. And all this without even going into the dangers about which so many scientists speak today, of annihilation or genetic perversion of the human race. In 1960 atomic war seems to me to raise for the Christian conscience not only a more urgent, but a radically different problem than did war in 1939. This is why pacifism has assumed for me and many others a new relevance, but in a very different perspective. This "neo-pacifism" is not rooted in the idealism of the old "absolute pacifism," which repudiated all other means of violent coercion along with war.

The neo-pacifism does not by principle repudiate violence as a means of political action. I can conceive of the valid use of armed force to stop local conflicts; I reject world war not because of its means but because of its foreseeable results. In other words, in this change in my attitude toward war I am not concerned only with the purity of my motivation or means, but also, and perhaps primarily, with the effectiveness of my action.

Is there a solution to this dilemma? Not if we are looking for some rules we can apply. Whether we choose purity at the cost of effectiveness, or effectiveness at the cost of purity, we stand guilty before God, and, in a positive sense, the conscientious objector renders as true a witness to Jesus Christ through his costly refusal of war as does the politician who uses devious means, or the revolutionary who is ready to kill and to destroy in order to wipe out intolerable injustice or oppression. Through the intervention of God, all may render Christian witness; but he alone can transform our imperfect obedience, so marred by disobedience, into an instrument of the manifestation of his love and glory. Our only concern is to render true witness, knowing that however noble our actions, we are always in need of his forgiveness. In the last analysis God alone bears witness to himself; we can only be unnecessary tools, but we must pray that he will use us in this way.

THE RISK

I speak here of the discernment of historical events which any political action presupposes. To engage in politics we first must know the world, analyze and evaluate the conjuncture of forces, take apart its wheels. Such evaluations must proceed from a person's historical judgment and as he examines situations and predicts results. They involve for us a terrible risk, for political blunders will make us responsible before God for injustice and suffering. Our good political intentions may well become the paving-stones of hell. But Christian life is lived by faith, not sight, and is always made up of these risks. Yet in the political realm they are more serious because of the enormous consequences these risks can have. But to refuse the risk is to refuse to accept the life of faith and to take refuge for example in the security of some set of rules, religious or secular, and this, as we have seen, contradicts the entire gospel.

It is God himself who requires us to run these risks, and this is the only reason we are able to assume them. For the Lord who commands is also the Saviour who forgives. As Christians we must make our decisions as wisely and honestly as we can, searching our faith and our knowledge of events, and then all we can do is to surrender to God the results of our choices, with the joyful conviction that our mistakes will not only be forgiven but even redeemed. Our decision will still remain terribly serious, because our life and the lives of our brothers are at stake. Yet regardless of what we have done or left undone, we know that Jesus Christ is our Lord and the Lord of our brothers, the Lord of the world, the only master of our destinies. Without this certitude we could never assume the appalling responsibility of war and peace, of economic or political action. For we cannot bear on our shoulders the burden of history, but thanks be to God, he has already taken it upon himself.

I turn again to my decision of 1939–40. What made me resolve then to accept war or revolutionary violence was the conviction that in making any other choice I would be deliberately disobeying Jesus Christ, ceasing to render witness to him. I do not claim, however, that all Christians should have done the same, and I maintain the highest respect for those who at the time chose pacifism or passive resistance. Since in the Christian ethic there is no political formula valid for all times and circumstances, we cannot rule out that equally faithful Christians in the same political situation will render witness to their Lord in different ways. And nothing authorizes us, when we have chosen the path of our obedience, to pass judgment on those whose faith leads them down different roads. Such divergencies are bound to raise problems about the unity of the church which we will have to consider later.

In any case, in making this choice I knew that it was for me the only possible one. How could I be so certain? Perhaps in the end I may not be able to explain it. In the Christian life there always come moments when one can no longer explain, but only affirm: "I can do no other. May God help me." In any case in 1940, as a citizen of a conquered country under military occupation, subjected to Hitlerian domination, I was absolutely certain that by coming to terms in any way with Nazi totalitarianism or its hired French regime, I would have betrayed far more than my political convictions. I would have betrayed my Christian faith. I would not only have acquiesced in injustice, oppression, and idolatry, I would have given a bad witness, or rather I would have witnessed not to the God of Jesus Christ, but to some false god of human invention, to the god of race, of power, of war. If I wanted to remain a faithful witness, my acts as well as my words had to prove that between Jesus Christ and the regime to which I was subject there was nothing in common. My political decision really came out of the concern about witness.

COMPROMISE

The dilemma between effectiveness and purity is encountered daily in politics. Any politician will confess that compromise is necessary. In order to reach positions of responsibility in political parties we must, to some extent, accept the rules of the political game, however sordid they may be. We must plunge into the smut of playing-up to personal ambitions and jealousies, of dispensing political patronage, of spreading propaganda, and so on. To refuse to get our hands dirty is to renounce forever the possibility of exerting effective influence. Even if the politician comes to power and enters the government, he will continue to run into the inevitable necessity for compromise, only on a larger scale. I have no intention whatever of debasing politicians. Even in France, where their reputation is anything but resplendent, they are perhaps more honest and conscientious, apart from a few notable exceptions, than we are usually willing to admit. But the fact remains that the rules of personal Christian ethics are obviously inapplicable to the political scene. Does anything go, then, in politics? I am once more up against the impossibility of giving any satisfactory answer, any gimmick to solve the dilemma. In the last analysis each one of us must take up his responsibilities, run his own risks before God. It is of course possible to eliminate the more scandalous forms of compromise. Never, for instance, can we justify a political compromise that merely serves our personal interests, especially financial ones. The problem may thereby be somewhat clarified, but it remains unresolved. The real issue is when not our personal interests but those of the community require us to compromise. There will always come the moment of decision between effectiveness and purity. Each time we must determine anew before God which obligation is to be given priority. Is it better to reject a too scandalous compromise and pay the price in political impotence, or to accept the compromise if it is apparently less costly to the community to be served than ineffectiveness? In this dilemma evangelism may be the only valid criterion. In each particular case we will have to ask ourselves whether we bear witness better by accepting ineffectiveness or by accepting compromise.

I would like to add here an observation and deplore, in fact, the present state of things. Christian politicians have good reason for complaining that the church in most cases abandons them. More than anyone else perhaps they are entitled to expect help from the church in the form of pastoral understanding and advice. All our churches should be encouraged to set up groups whose only responsibility would be to gather together in support of Christian politicians, to talk with them of the manifold political and spiritual problems they have to face, without wishing to dictate any solution, to provide the moral support and practical counsel that they need, and, above all, to give them pastoral care. As much as politicians resent what they call "interference of the church" in technical questions beyond its competence, they nevertheless would welcome, I think, such an initiative as this. To judge from my own personal reminiscence as a French cabinet officer for some months, the politician does not ask the church to do his job in his place. Rather, he wants the church to be for him the community where he can hear the Word of God, receive the pastoral ministry he needs, and share with his fellow believers the difficulties and the joys of Christian life.

One last remark about political parties. Seen in the missionary perspective which is ours, political parties not only are the means of an effective witness. They provide in addition the opportunity for continuous contacts with people who share our struggle but not our faith. I know of no better occasion for Christian witness. To struggle together, to be dedicated to a common cause, to act and to run risks together creates far more vivid bonds between people that a simple encounter does. If I may recall again my engagement in the Resistance, I don't think I have elsewhere experienced such richness in the exchange of thoughts and confidence between men who did not hold the same faith. Rarely have I come upon so many occasions for true and natural witness. I am convinced that participation in a political party offers comparable possibilities to the Christian.

V. THE DISTINCTIVE MARKS OF CHRISTIAN INVOLVEMENT

I would like to point out some special characteristics that mark the political involvement of the Christian, whatever form it takes.

HUMOR AND SERIOUSNESS

When we undertake to act politically we should do so with a certain humor. God demands that we love our fellow men as he has loved them in Jesus Christ. Because through politics we can love our neighbor and witness to Jesus Christ, our political responsibility has a seriousness and urgency which even the greatest human zeal could not give it. But we need not be anxious. Some years ago a Communist, speaking of his struggle for peace, said, "Please understand, you Christians, that for us the situation is far more tragic than for you. We know nothing except history. If you fail you still have your hope for another world. If we fail, we are left with empty hands and without hope." This Communist, in spite of his oversimplification, had understood the Christian approach to politics. It is true that our hope of the Kingdom delivers us from despair, encourages us to engage in politics without anxiety, enables us to struggle with a certain sense of humor: for our human efforts, effective or ineffective, cannot change Christ's victory. He rules over the world, he uses us to manifest his Lordship, yet nothing, not even our failures and betrayals, can prevent his continuing to reign from the beginning of the world until eternity.

OPTIMISM AND REALISM

Thus our attitude can be a strange mixture of political realism, sometimes very pessimistic, and of fundamental optimism. We have no illusions about the world and its desperate plight—Jesus Christ died because of it. We have no illusions either about our human capacity to improve the world. Nevertheless a profound optimism inspires us. We are optimists because we await the return of our Lord, because we know that the world has no other future than the Kingdom of God. We can even go beyond this optimism about the final end of things. We can even be optimistic about our present struggles; if we try to fulfill God's will, to be his instruments, we can even be hopeful about immediate political results. For we know that all political hopes of mankind, all the projects of reform and reconstruction reflect, without knowing it, something of the glory of God. We can therefore make them our own, commit ourselves joyously to them with a certain optimism, since they accord with the will of the Lord, a Lord who will come again at the last but who right now rules over the nations and works among men. This is strange optimism, since it is not based on the certainty of success, but on the pure joy of knowing that we are in the service of God, co-workers with him.

HOPE, POLITICAL ACTION, AND WITNESS

The last characteristic of the Christian who engages in political action is that he does so knowing that he remains an unprofitable servant, that the destiny of the world depends on God alone, that his Kingdom is at hand, and that its coming does not depend at all on the success of our efforts. This is probably the most disconcerting of all aspects of our eschatological hope for those who have not yet understood it. Why get involved, why fight, if the future of the world depends on God alone? Why not simply wait for the glorious day of the Kingdom? Why not fall back into quietism? This is really the permanent question that mankind always asks of God. It is man's reaction to the free gift of salvation. Nothing is more paradoxical than Paul's formulation, "work out your own salvation with fear and trembling; since it is God who produces in you the willing and the doing" (Phil. 2:12–13). God does everything; our salvation, the salvation of the world, depend only on him. But this does not entitle us to conclude that we have nothing to do. Perhaps to understand the relation between God's all-sufficient action and our human responsibility, we would have to put ourselves in God's place, and this is precisely what we must not and cannot do.

Without going further into the theological question here, let us take up two images that may help us to understand why quietism is an impossibility for us. They are related to gratitude and witness. Before God, we are like children who have discovered that their father loves them no matter what they do. Shall they then disobey him and remain deaf to his orders? Of course not. They will want to respond to his love with grateful love of their own and a desire to please him. For the Christian, gratitude is the real motive for responsible action. It helps to understand why eschatological hope and political action do not contradict each other.

Another helpful image is the familiar modern parable used by so many Christian writers since the Second World War. When in 1944 the Allied forces were successful in landing troops on the beaches of Normandy, all of us in the occupied countries in Western Europe who heard of it knew that the end of the war was approaching and that the decisive victory was won. But we were still under Nazi occupation. What did we do? Give up the Resistance and fold our hands, waiting for the Liberation to come? Far from it! The victory of the Normandy beaches was the signal for general insurrection. People fought with new vigor and enthusiasm against the enemy who still occupied the country. But it was a different fight, still dangerous, but victorious. Above all we spread the news of the victory among those who had not yet heard it and called them to join in the battle. The great fame this parable has rightly achieved in the course of the last decade is due to its astonishing meaningfulness and precision. I for one know of no more striking description of the situation of the Christian between the resurrection and the return of the Lord. True, the resurrection guarantees his return, assures us that God's victory and our salvation are no illusion. But this certitude is precisely what makes us understand the urgency and the meaning of our human activities, of our political engagement in particular, as well as its missionary significance. Not only must we fight the battle against the Prince of this world in a rear-guard action. We are above all called to make known to all men the splendid news of their liberation which they have not yet heard or do not yet believe. On that June morning in 1944, when we heard the news of the landing in Normandy, our joy was so great that we went about telling it to everyone, to friends and strangers alike. As Christians we are the privileged few who know the wonderful news. We cannot but proclaim it everywhere through our words and our struggle. The time of Christ's victory is the time of our responsibility, the time for witness.

I would like to quote here one of the great Christian maxims that best sums up what I have tried to say. It is the motto of William the Silent: "It is not necessary to hope in order to undertake, nor to succeed in order to persevere." We do not need to succeed, or to hope to succeed, in order to act politically, because we have a better hope. To this hope all our political action must witness.

VI. POLITICAL ACTION AND EVANGELISTIC CONFRONTATION

The Christian is constantly tempted to obey for the sake of obedience, to witness for the sake of being faithful, to act politically for the sake of fulfilling a duty; in brief, to live in a constant search for purity—as if purity could be found elsewhere than in the free gift of Jesus Christ. But, in so doing, the Christian neglects the other motivation of Christian witness and action: meeting man's needs, service to our neighbor, and concern for his life and faith.

Are Christians so prone to take this self-centered attitude because of a deep and genuine fear of the world, of being confronted with its questions, of engaging it in conversation, in dialogue? I have tried to show that this dialogue is essential to evangelism. I want now to explain briefly how it can happen in political life.

We fall so easily into a deadly monologue because we lack faith and, above all, hope. In recent years there has been a great effort to rediscover the biblical meaning of hope. The World Council of Churches chose this as the theme of its 1954 Assembly: "Jesus Christ, the hope of the world." Do we really believe what we say? Have we worked out our theological convictions in terms of our ethical and missionary responsibility in the world? Even though we affirm that Jesus Christ is the hope of the world, we behave as if there were hope for only a sort of residual world, an empty shell from which everything "worldly" has been carefully removed. We speak of Jesus Christ as the hope of the world. Does this mean that he is the hope of nationalism and communism, of science and art, of philosophies, ideologies, and religions, that he is the hope of all men and women with their political and religious convictions? Quite honestly, isn't your answer no, Jesus Christ is the hope of the Communist *in spite of* his communism, of the nationalist *in spite of* his nationalism, of the scientist *in spite of* his science, of the Buddhist *in spite of* Buddhism? I am not able to explain how Jesus Christ can be the hope of communism, nationalism, science, or Buddhism, and perhaps we are not allowed even to raise the question. But one thing I know: we must not proclaim to these men and women that Jesus Christ is *their hope* in terms that would require them to give up everything they think, do, love, and hope. If a Communist cannot hear the good news of Jesus Christ without having first given up his communism, if the Christian message is meaningless for the nationalist as long as he is a nationalist, for the socialist or the conservative as long as they are socialist or conservative, Jesus Christ can have no meaning for men and women in their human situation. And in a sense this is also theologically true: Jesus Christ can have no meaning for men and women without the miracle of the Holy Spirit. But this miracle reaches them at the very center of their humanity. The Holy Spirit does reach them; but what of our witness, and the witness of our churches? How often have the churches cut themselves off from genuine encounter with the world by taking an attitude of superiority or indifference, by refusing to concern themselves with what men live for?

And now a second question: do we really believe that men and women in the world around us can become Christians, can be converted? Why is the word "conversion" so commonly left to sectarian groups or aged sentimentalists, and so little used in our churches? There are probably historical reasons for this reluctance to use a good biblical term, especially the way in which it has been misused in the past. But there is also, perhaps, something more serious, another aspect of the purity-effectiveness tension. Is the reason we are often so concerned with our own purity that, at heart, we do not believe that people can be converted? Our churches, especially in the Western world, have too long been static. For too long they have ceased to expand. Their main concern today is to preserve Christians from the dangerous contagion of unbelief, or, at best, to win back those who have lapsed. There are few who fully believe in the Holy Spirit and thus see the whole world as the parish of the Church.

Can we convert people? Of course not; no man has ever been able to do so. When someone, through our witness, comes to believe, it is God himself who grants him faith, and we are only unprofitable servants. The crucial factor is God's decision and promise to love the world, which nothing will ever change. God has spoken once for all and his Word is Jesus Christ, present in the world and for the world from eternity to eternity. There is therefore a real hope for the world; because Jesus Christ is this hope, all men are promised salvation and called to faith, and for all, faith is a real possibility. Therefore we must preach, we must witness to Jesus Christ through our whole life with the great expectation that, in spite of all obstacles, our own unworthiness and the unworthiness of all men, the Word of God will be heard, believed, and obeyed. Conversion is a possibility, and therefore our task. But what can we do for the conversion of others?

In the first place, and precisely because their conversion is God's action, we must pray for it. Unless we pray that they may be given faith, our witness is mere words. Secondly, we must witness to Jesus Christ, not to ourselves. At every point we must make clear our own unimportance and His supreme importance. Thirdly, we must love our neighbor and really meet him and know him well enough so we can speak of Jesus Christ to him, and not to some imaginary figure.

How does this apply to political action? Let us note first that political action facilitates human confrontation. The links established by a common struggle in which everyone runs the same risks are strong and vital. When we have been on the same battlefield, political or military, when we have fought together against the same evil and joined forces in the same social program, we belong together; we have fellowship with one another and can speak together more easily than is usually possible. Political action establishes a sort of kinship between men which is not evangelism but which facilitates it greatly. I am speaking here out of personal experience in underground activities: our contacts with people who shared our political struggle but not our faith, were wonderful human experiences and real missionary opportunities.

It is not enough, however, to rely on the normal opportunities provided by political action for individual Christians. The church itself should look for such opportunities, should initiate the dialogue with the world, especially with political groups. Over the last years, the World's Student Christian Federation has had conversations with the International Union of Students, a body under strong Communist influence. We were first asked by the IUS to meet with them to explain our attitude on current political affairs and particularly our refusal to support Communist-inspired peace campaigns. I well remember our first hesitations. We could so easily imagine the reactions which such conversations would provoke, both within and outside the Christian community. We finally agreed because "it is a matter of Christian witness always to be ready to speak to those who ask us to do so." Especially in our day "conversation with an organization which represents primarily students in Communist-controlled areas is a real way of keeping the door open between hostile parts of the world, while refusing it would in some way contribute to building up the 'iron curtain.'" "While the possible results of such a meeting should be looked at realistically, as Christians we should always be open to the possibility of what we call a miracle, that is to say, the grace of God working through us in ways we could not reasonably expect."[2]

The major reason for our accepting the proposition of IUS was without doubt the opportunity for witness that such an encounter held out. To discuss peace, in 1955, with Communists was perhaps politically useful. When the world is so sharply divided that even discussion between the rival power blocs becomes difficult or totally ceases, any contact across the Iron or Bamboo Curtain takes on exceptional significance. Isolation creates ignorance; ignorance creates fear; and fear is always pregnant with violence. Any dialogue across this wall of silence is therefore precious. Even if these conversations do not make any evident progress toward solving the great political questions, the simple encounter helps to dispel prejudices, sometimes even to build up mutual respect that cannot but work in favor of international relaxation. But in any case, our first concern was a missionary one. We had agreed to speak with them about peace, because we saw in this an exceptional opportunity to proclaim Jesus Christ. In an age of cold war and international tension, how could a Christian talk of peace without referring to the Prince of Peace? The political problem of international peace can surely provide a remarkable vocabularly for witness.

What about the results of these conversations? God alone knows whether or not his Word was heard, but I remember moments in our sessions, and even more in personal conversations, when I had the impression that, as we talked of political matters and even of our most profound human convictions, we were expressing, in terms of the concern which had brought us together, something of Jesus Christ's love for his world and of our hope for another day when everything will be new and there will be peace forever. I remember the moving moment when one of our Communist friends told us that, for the first time, he had been compelled to look at himself in an effort to discover his ultimate commitment, the meaning of his life. I have no doubt about the evangelistic significance of such conversations.

One of the essential conditions for real encounter is, of course, that as Christians we do not come with a spirit of controversy, to win points in a political argument, but rather to speak with people whom we wish and need to meet in spite of our disagreements; with

[2] From "The Minutes of a Meeting of the WSCF Officers," January, 1951.

the desire to learn as well as to teach. If we desire encounter for
the sake of witness, we must be genuinely interested in other people.
We may criticize their convictions but, however radical and valid our
criticism, it must not rule out human sympathy for the people
across the table, for the dignity with which they try to live up to
their convictions, right or wrong, even sympathy for those convictions in which we can often recognize evidence that God has not
abandoned the world. One word encompasses all this: openness.
The secret of evangelism is to be open to everything human and
to say with the philosopher, but in another sense: "Nothing human
is foreign to me." Nothing human can be foreign to the Christian
because in Jesus Christ the whole of mankind, with all its greatness
and its weakness, is present. When we meet non-Christians with
such openness, something happens for which we cannot account:
the mystery of the presence, between two men confronting each
other and trying to speak together, of a third invisible Person who
makes the dialogue meaningful by adding his own words in his own
way.

We spoke with the IUS about peace, and all Christian partici-
pants in the conversations expressed their political convictions on
current international problems. We often disagreed among ourselves.
It is significant that this disagreement among Christians, far from
weakening our effort, made it perhaps more effective by showing
that, as Christians, we were united not by a common political concern, but by something transcending all political concerns. Our disagreement on political issues manifested our unity in faith, and
was in itself an evangelistic affirmation.

It also helped us to overcome the danger of self-righteousness and
compelled us to humility, to a recognition of our own shortcomings.
In such dialogues with the world nothing is more dangerous than
to approach other men with a sense of superiority. When we do so,
dialogue becomes impossible, or is limited to mere political controversy. In such political conversations we must achieve two seemingly contradictory purposes; we must speak as those who take politics with the utmost seriousness—otherwise the dialogue remains
very superficial—but we must also be concerned with something
beyond politics, with the life, conversion, and faith of our inter-
locutors. Only in humility can the contradiction disappear: a political dialogue can be an evangelistic encounter if we know that our
task is not to win a victory for God, but to listen together with

others to the news of God's victory, which condemns and forgives us all.

A last word about conversion. I have said that in political life we should never lose sight of our goal, the conversion of all men. We must also recognize the political implications of evangelism and conversion. When a person believes, something changes in the world, even the world of politics. I am not speaking here of the gradual Christianization of the world; I simply mean that political disorder is rooted in human sin. At the end, when Christ returns in glory, there will be no more sin and political disorder will disappear. Each time someone believes, the coming Kingdom is present in the world, and this is bound to have political results, as the history of foreign mission shows. We should not fall into the pietistic error of thinking that political action is unnecessary and that only preaching matters; I have tried to show that without political action evangelism is incomplete and distorted. But we should not forget either that political action, however effective and successful it may be, will not solve the problems of the world, and has no real significance for the world if it does not contribute to evangelism.

CHAPTER VI

The Ministry of Reconciliation

So far I have dealt with the personal involvement of the Christian in politics. I would now like to go back to the Church. It is indeed impossible to limit the Church's responsibility to its public pronouncement without seriously curtailing it. True, the Church speaks; but it also lives. Its very existence has a prophetic meaning, a missionary dimension. The Church can serve the world by other means than words.

I. THE CHURCH IN A DIVIDED WORLD

THE WORLD OF FEAR

The world in which we live, act politically, and bear witness is a divided world. We suffer daily from the consequences of this division: international tensions, class struggle, racial discrimination and segregation, economic competition, all are highly political expressions of this division. But politics also affect our most intimate personal relationships. Its passions, which divide national and local communities, all too frequently creep into the circle of the family, destroying friendships, imperiling the unity of the Church. As philosophers and sociologists have often noted, the essential ill from which contemporary society suffers is that men no longer know how to live together. I have already mentioned that our century passionately seeks for a social ethic, for a way of living together. In the background of all the uncertainties we run into the essential problem: that of encounter, of meeting another human being. It is well worth while to have some familiarity with existential literature, for more profoundly than anything else it reflects the crisis of our time. It has emphasized a fundamental psychological and social phenomenon: for modern man, "the other" represents a threat, a frightening unknown. When someone looks at me, meets me, my existence is called in question; I cease to be a subject; he makes me an object; I lose my freedom. This psychological analysis has its sociological counterpart. In an increasingly complex world where the individual is caught in a web of dependence, both economic and political, is there any room left for liberty in the traditional sense of the word? Or must we look elsewhere for a new concept of collective life, for new values that would come to take the place of liberty? In politics as well as in philosophy Sartre's formulation is relevant: "Hell is other people."

This fear of others, this incapacity to live together, poisons all human relationships, accounts for inward tensions and practical problems. Fear conditions international relations as well as the relations of classes and races, giving them a panicky and irrational character which makes for the gravity of the present political crisis. The fear of Americans about Russian communism borders on mystical horror, and the same may be said of the terror of the Communist world regarding America. In racial conflicts ethnic groups have an irrational terror of one another. In social struggles workers and employers impute to one another almost demonic intentions and powers. This irrational fear gives to contemporary politics a passionate and unredeemable aspect; when men fear, they cease to think; they attack without calculating the risk and the cost of their haste, because they are afraid of being attacked. Violence becomes almost inevitable, whether as wars, strikes, revolutions, race riots, or the ostracisms that today breed in the concentration camps and the refugee centers.

NONTHEOLOGICAL FACTORS IN THE DIVISION OF THE CHURCH

Bewailing our plight does not help; we must act. These fears, this violence, summon the church to action, to witness, to works of love. And this is all the more urgent as the church itself suffers from these divisions. The great ecumenical movement of the twentieth century, which has emphasized the confessional and theological divisions, has more recently undertaken an analysis of the "nontheological factors" that break or threaten the unity of the church. But this study has investigated the causes of institutional divisions and neglected the hidden schisms that pervert Christian unity within each denomination, even each congregation. Can there be Christian unity when racial segregation penetrates the structure of the congregation? When we tolerate that rich and poor live side by side in the church without our offering anything more than a sometimes patronizing charity to remedy the most shocking misery? When political factions cannot sit together in the same church except by carefully avoiding controversial subjects? When the national churches speak out on great current issues without prior consultation with one another? The seriousness of these divisions within the church can never be emphasized too much for, although not reflected in official church structures, they create chasms of suspicion among Christians. When a war leads Christians, weapons in hand, onto a battlefield to fight and perhaps kill one another, the Body of Christ is as deeply wounded as it is by confessional anarchy, and perhaps more deeply. As Christians we are members of one Body, and this must be true not only of our ecclesiastical relation but of all our life, not only on Sunday morning but on every day of the week. The unity of the Church requires that we condemn everything that separates Christians.

In this judicial process the church is not only on the side of the prosecution; it also sits among the accused. For in its own way it helps to proliferate and aggravate human divisions. Quite apart from the way in which Christians and their churches take part in political conflicts, they are guilty of creating tensions themselves, such as for example, the political tensions which result from the conflicts between Catholics and Protestants. The persecution which the Roman Catholic Church so often tolerates, when it is not directly responsible for it, affects not only ecclesiastical relations but constitutes an element in international and social disorder.

Protestantism moreover cannot take refuge in a good conscience that is spiritually pernicious and historically unjustified. It is not so very long since Catholics first obtained equal civil rights in Protestant countries, and in many cases still they do not yet enjoy these rights fully. What part has the shameless proselytism of many confessional groups played in creating the climate of suspicion and violence which prevails in various parts of the world, the Middle East for instance? The confessional political parties, in dragging the church onto the political stage, inflame the ideological and international conflicts, tending to transform them into religious wars. Our churches bear a heavy share of the responsibility for the two great conflicts of our time: the first is the cold war between the Communist world and the Western world, which the churches are constantly in danger of turning into a crusade; the second, the tension between the Bandoeng powers and the imperialistic powers, whatever form their domination may take. I discussed earlier the ambiguities of the nineteenth-century missionary movement, and its political repercussions. Developments in the last few years have done nothing to mitigate these. The church thus finds itself in the very center of the political whirlwind, of all the divisions of the modern world. It contributes to them as much as it suffers from them. What then can it do to heal them?

A GIVEN UNITY

The unity of the Church—this is the very foundation of all ecumenical thinking—is rooted outside the Church, in the reconciling and redeeming act of Jesus Christ. Whatever the divisions that plague the church, its unity is a *fact*, is a part of revelation. The New Testament teaching is clear: the Church is one by nature, since it is the Body of Christ; it has a given unity. Its division is not merely scandalous, it is unthinkable, inconceivable. As Christians we must believe and confess this unity and catholicity of the Church; we must learn to recognize it behind all our theological, confessional, or political divergences; we must pray for it, beseeching God to make it visible again. We must do everything in our power to overcome the divisions and find new ways of showing our oneness.

The christological character of our unity forbids us to seek it in any human agreement, in any political alignment, in administrative centralization, or even in any theological uniformity. The church cannot recover the knowledge and the practice of its unity except by faith in the Head of the Church, by repentance, obedience, and witness. We must be especially watchful of the danger of administrative centralization. We should thank God that the World Council of Churches, certainly one of the most significant efforts toward unity, has so far steered clear of this reef; it would be disastrous were the World Council to be transformed into some sort of super-church, even if it achieved impressive results on the level of organization, efficiency, and prestige, for this would have nothing to do with the real unity of the Body of Christ. The church cannot come together except in following its Lord, in the weakness of the cross, and not in the worldly glory that Satan offered to Jesus when he tempted him in the wilderness. This unity must operate at the local level as well as in ecumenical relationships, in matters of doctrine as well as of practice. Above all, this unity must reflect the image of our Lord: the unity of the Church must speak to the world of the Suffering Servant and not of some glorious human achievement; it must proclaim Jesus Christ's resurrection, but not apart from his cross.

II. PERSONAL INVOLVEMENT AND UNITY
   OF THE CHURCH

How will this fundamental unity of the Church be manifested in the political realm? I have said that it is permissible, even natural, that Christians choose different roads and join parties with conflicting programs in order to express their obedience in the field of politics. There is nothing shocking in this. But such variety does run the danger of provoking divisions within the Church, and we must be viligant lest our conflicting political commitments destroy our oneness in faith. I shall refer once again to my experience in the French Resistance movement. I was then a member of the French Student Christian Movement. Most of us had become active members of the underground; some, however, had decided for passive resistance, while a few, without falling prey to Nazi idolatry, refused to condemn the Vichy government in which they saw some merit. Our Student Christian Movement was threatened with division by these different political choices. What did we do? First, the French SCM carefully avoided adopting any official political line. It never spoke publicly, except on issues where the integrity of the Christian faith was at stake, such as anti-Semitism or the deportation of students to Germany under the pretext of compulsory labor service. Otherwise it remained silent, not through fear of the police, but because it was convinced that concrete political decisions rested with each individual member and not with the movement as a whole. Did this mean that in our meetings we avoided all the burning and disputed questions? Far from it! Hardly a week passed when we did not try to meet our personal differences face to face, criticizing one another and learning not only from those with whom we agreed, but also from those who understood their obedience differently. Our conversations were often hard, painful; our convictions clashed violently. The very subject matter of our controversies gave them a harsh but also a serious character. Yet in most cases there was real exchange within the community of the church and not mere political debates. There were exceptions, to be sure, and our discussions sometimes ruptured relationships. Yet by and large our unity was safeguarded. Had we tried to preserve it by avoiding controversial subjects we would have run a far greater risk of division. For any unity maintained by this policy of silence would have been empty of any real content, a unity of appearances without any real meaning.

MUTUAL CORRECTION

There can be no unity in the church without this difficult and sometimes painful confrontation between the conflicting political positions of its members. The nature of the Church requires this openness. We are members of the Church with our whole being. To limit our Christian life to "religious questions" is to deny that Jesus Christ has redeemed our entire existence. If the church should avoid political controversies and concentrate only on questions of theology, of spiritual life, or of personal morals, it would only display its lack of faith; it would implicitly affirm that God has nothing to do with politics, that politics is outside the bounds of salvation, that the Lordship of Christ is merely "spiritual." The church would fall into the pietist fallacy, making of the gospel a promise which is not offered to the world, but only to those who have broken with the world; even the gospel of God's grace would be lost.

The church must therefore be vigilant and call its members to exercise the ministry of mutual criticism and correction, taking the initiative itself if necessary. Each local congregation should make provisions for such confrontations, for example in political study groups which would apply themselves to the analysis of current issues, especially those which raise difficult problems of conscience or endanger Christian unity. Christians engaged in politics could here keep informed about the thinking of the church. Whereas some specialists try to keep abreast with the principal church pronouncements and theological studies relating to social, international, and economic questions, the rank and file of church members remain indifferent, not because of lack of interest, but through lack of information. Such political study groups should not be limited to the task of becoming informed. Their members should also engage in a common effort to think through the political demands of their faith and prepare themselves through mutual correction for a more faithful witness, whose integrity, far from endangering the unity of the church, will enrich it.

ECUMENICAL UNITY

I wish also to underline the importance of confrontation and mutual correction at the national and interdenominational level. Much has already been achieved. I have already referred to the Commission of the Churches on International Affairs, and I could cite a number of bilateral conversations. But there is still much to be done. Too often these interchurch conversations are somewhat artificial confrontations of political or theological experts, "summit meetings" about which the great majority of Christians are very little concerned. With rare exceptions, Christians still think of political problems in a strictly national framework, even when international questions are at issue. I was made sadly aware of this sort of ecclesiastical nationalism which so many French Protestants showed at the time of the Suez crisis in 1956. It marked first of all a lack of interest in Christian opinion in the rest of the world, but also a sharp reaction against Christians in other countries who criticized French policy and who were accused of interfering in something which did not concern them. I can't help condemning such nationalism as scandalous. As Christians we should never call "foreign" those who share our faith. If we truly believe in what we confess in the Apostles' Creed, that the Church is *one*, then we cannot allow national frontiers to introduce even the least separation. Our faith binds us to our fellow believers, to all those who share it, whatever their nationality or their political convictions, much more closely than to any national or political community. We are responsible one for the other in the community of the Church in a fashion far more immediate and profound than we can ever be for our fellow citizens or co-workers in a political party.

This interdependence in the Church, however, does not permit us to make decisions for one another. Each one of us remains personally responsible before God at that place where God has put us. Christian obedience is always concrete obedience, here and now. It would be both dangerous and vain to legislate for one another, even within the Church. I have always found it a risky undertaking when the churches in Europe, America, or Asia have attempted to prescribe what the churches in South Africa should do about racial matters. Only the South African Christians themselves can assume before God the risk of their choice. To decide from outside, theoretically, would be as ridiculous as to sit in judgment on the church's position at the time of Constantine or in the Middle Ages. It serves no purpose to wish to rewrite history, and we have no right to judge the faithfulness of our brothers. On the other hand, Christians everywhere should feel responsible to speak with their brothers about the problems they face in a desire for mutual correction and counselling, and of course mutual correction is a two-way process. It is probable that such a conversation would be more concerned with fundamental Christian ethics than with technical solutions for the South African race problem; it would be more of a biblical and theological discussion than a political one. But this does not matter; what is essential is that the confrontation takes place, and, above all, that it takes place within the fellowship of the Church, in a climate of genuine mutual respect, confidence, and prayer, where the South African church can count on the criticism and support of their brothers in the ecumenical fellowship.

But the search for the unity of the church must not be limited to attempts at correction on the theological and ethical level. Intellectual exchanges must go hand in hand with all forms of interchurch aid. Intercession, above all else, is the condition of unity. There is no Christian faithfulness without prayer, and there is no unity of the church without intercession.

COMMON ACTION

Thus far I have spoken only of conversations and mutual correction. What about common action? If we rule out Christian political parties and emphasize the personal character of political involvement, must we conclude that Christians are left always to act in isolation? Without contradicting the preceding chapter it seems to

me that there is room for Christian co-operation even in the field
of common action. I cannot make a case for political effectiveness
and then deny the importance of working together. We shall of
course need to be cautious lest we fall back into the error of Christian
political parties. But it is entirely admissible, even desirable, that
Christians go into battle together, and not dispersed. To take another illustration from French politics; several years ago, in a rural
area, some Protestants decided to undertake a common effort of
renewal in the political life of the region and, with this intent,
joined the same political party. Because there were many of them,
they managed to gain control of the regional political machine and
to change its leadership. But they carefully avoided placing one of
their group at the head of the machine, for had they done so, they
might have given the impression of a confessional invasion of party
politics. On the contrary, they managed to be politically effective
without using ambiguous methods. This effort seems to have had not
only political results but also a missionary significance: new contacts
were established with non-Christian circles, new opportunities created for evangelism, and the good news of Jesus Christ preached
in a new and significant way.

Much more could be said about the significance of the unity of the
church from the point of view of both politics and evangelism. Jesus
Christ has promised that unity would serve the missionary cause and
his words have become an ecumenical watchword: "that all may be
one that the world may believe." But have we applied the promise
also to unity at the political level? I have tried to give some illustrations from the political realms of the unity—not uniformity—of
the church. We have the promise of Jesus Christ that when such
unity is achieved people will hear and believe. This is another way
of emphasizing that, in our efforts toward unity, we must be concerned with Jesus Christ and not with ourselves, that we must
seek unity for its own sake and aim only to manifest Jesus Christ,
the Head of the Body we constitute together.

We must also watch that this Body, the Church, be an open
community. "That all may be one that the world may believe": our
unity is a unity prepared for the world, incomplete as long as the
world refuses to join it, a unity which constantly sends us into the
world with a message of invitation. Concern for unity among churches
and Christians must therefore be accompanied by concern for the
unity of the world. It is part of our mission to overcome both our

inner divisions and divisions among nations, classes, races, among men. But these efforts toward secular unity cannot be separated from our faith in, and struggle for, the unity of the church. Indeed, the unity of the church should be our first contribution to unity among men. When the church is one, in doctrine and thinking, in mutual assistance and love, in structure and relations, one also in its political understanding and obedience, the Kingdom of Christ is present. The church will never be more than analogous to the Kingdom and its unity will always be imperfect; but each step toward unity, each common act, is surely a sign to the world of the perfect unity of all things and all men in the love of Jesus Christ, in his Kingdom. This proclamation of the Kingdom through our unity is an evangelistic, missionary service, but also a political act. It is proof to the world that for men something else is possible than hatred, fear, and suspicion. The unity of the church is a sign of the coming Kingdom: it can also be a model for political relationships. When churches help one another through a program of mutual assistance across national frontiers, they provide an example to the United Nations of help given with no strings attached. When churches from both sides of the Iron Curtain make the painful effort to face their deep political differences, to speak about them frankly, and to love one another in spite of them, they show the world that in Jesus Christ there is a power which transcends East and West, and also, very concretely, that conversation across the Curtain is not only possible but fruitful. Or, to take an example at the local level, there is a political as well as an evangelistic value in all efforts to organize Christian co-operatives.

In brief, when the church, through repentance for its division and longing for unity manifests that it is the Church of Jesus Christ, something new and powerful is at work in the world of politics. Totalitarian powers have sometimes understood this more quickly than Christians themselves, and have persistently opposed all real manifestations of church unity.

IS RECONCILIATION POSSIBLE?

We are one because Christ has reconciled us one with another; we preach Jesus Christ the Reconciler, and from him we have received the ministry of reconciliation. But can we reconcile? Can we hope for international relations based on unity and love? I do not think so. Not that war should be inevitable, but reconciliation is not of this world; it is the mark of the Kingdom of God and a sign of the Church in this world. But between war and true reconciliation lie many possible solutions. Which should we choose? Even though it is politically and emotionally "loaded," I rather like the term "peaceful co-existence." I do not advocate use of the Communist slogan, but I must recognize that in international affairs peaceful co-existence is a rather good "analogy" of the reconciliation characteristic of the Kingdom and of the Church.

God does not permit either war or full unity. From the first pages of the Bible he forbids violence and murder, and even puts a sign on Cain, the murderer, to protect him from retaliation. But when men sought unity around the tower of Babel, he scattered them, and by creating a confusion of tongues, raised a barrier against such future attempts. Henceforth human unity was only part of the eschatological hope: in Abraham, all nations of the earth will be one, and their kings will bring tribute to the Lamb in the heavenly Jerusalem; in the Kingdom of God nations will be reconciled and, in a sense, are already reconciled on earth within the Church of the Pentecost. Our world remains under the threat of division and war, but God does not permit its annihilation.

Until Christ's second coming, nations will therefore co-exist without being able to unite, and the task of the church will be to call them to a co-existence, which is really peaceful, which resembles the ultimate reconciliation of the Kingdom. However peaceful this co-existence, it will always remain provisional and imperfect, a challenge to our obedience rather than a cause for satisfaction. We can neither accept international relations based on the law of the jungle, nor escape into an irresponsible dream of world government, nor be satisfied with "cold-war" co-existence in which there is no peace. Real peace is not the absence of war. Perhaps one of the problems of international relations is that too much attention is given to preventing war and too little to building peace. It is, of course, understandable that statesmen, faced with the threat of atomic war, do everything to avoid it through schemes for the effective control of disarmament, the punishment of aggression, through the delimitation of zones of influence for the great powers, and other steps devised to maintain the *status quo*. But what are they doing to promote co-operation between rival nations, an equally urgent and perhaps more fruitful field of action? How reluctant are the great powers to associate themselves in a common program of technical or economic assistance to underdeveloped countries. How ridiculous is the United Nations' budget for technical assistance when compared with the astronomic sums spent by even the smallest nations for military preparations! What a miserable show of political ineptitude is given by the great powers when they argue endlessly about political conditions before granting help to countries in need! Programs of international assistance, which could be the basis for a really peaceful co-existence, become additional factors of tension. Here again the church has a task and an opportunity. I have already cited the example of interchurch aid. If I may risk the application to the field of international relations of a well-known ecumenical definition, I would say that the church should teach that "we should do together everything which our conscience does not compel us to do separately."

This the church can also do through direct participation in political affairs. Here I would make an exception to the rule that action is the task of the individual Christian and not of the church. But how can the church actually promote peaceful co-existence among nations or social groups? How can the church, for instance, help improve relations between Israel and Arab nations, between Western powers and their former colonies, perhaps even between the Western and the Communist blocs? The church can only fulfill such a ministry if it has guarded its freedom and avoided identification with one of the conflicting parties. Our churches might have done more in the great East-West struggle if, on both sides, they had preserved their independence. But I want to give some positive illustrations of how this task can be fulfilled. At the present time, in a great university center, a Student Christian Movement is trying to bring together students from Israel and from Arab countries. This effort may or may not succeed, but it has been possible because both sides recognized that the Christian students were fair, open-minded, and free from a selfish desire for success and power. Another example is that of the excellent initiative taken some years ago by a leader of the Commission of the Churches on International Affairs at a time when negotiations for an armistice in Korea seemed to be deadlocked; by proposing to the negotiators a new and untried solution, he contributed greatly to the ultimate success of the armistice. Any expert on diplomacy could have done the same, but this church leader took international problems sufficiently seriously to make this great effort of thought and imagination, and the diplomats concerned respected him enough to listen to him in a time of need.

CONCLUSION

Our political responsibility is human and relative. My last example shows rather well its human character, for our task is not to introduce into political life a religious climate, but to engage in politics in a creative way. It calls for integrity, freedom from partisan bias, expert "know-how," and, as I have said, much imagination. This is very "down-to-earth," but our responsibility is down-to-earth because it concerns the daily existence of men, nations, and societies. It demands that we be fully human, sharing the life of men, their misery and their greatness, their fears and their hopes. By accepting this down-to-earth political task, by avoiding all idealistic dreams, we shall serve men at the point of their suffering, and also show them something of the Kingdom of Christ. Only in this way will politics become a language for evangelism.

Finally, politics has only a relative importance. It can be the language of evangelism, and there is no evangelism without political content and political implications. But let us never forget that the real weapon of the Church is the gospel itself. Some years ago, in a discussion about the threat of persecution, a well-known Christian leader said, "When persecution threatens, the church must do three things. On the political plane, it must fight for a good political and social order free of all persecution. It must strengthen its faith and unity so that, when the evil days come, it can withstand the storm. But above all, faced with the offensive of the world, it must itself take the offensive, armed with the gospel." Unless the church knows this, there is no evangelism and no Christian political responsibility. The fulfillment of both our political and missionary duties depends on our knowledge that God has given us an arm which is more powerful than all the arms of the world. It is the conviction that the victory which overcomes the world is our faith that Jesus Christ is the Son of God (I John 4, 5). In the power of this conviction, in the power of God's word, the church will find strength and vision to face its task in the world, and to render true witness through politics.